on
gratitude

Sheryl Crow, Jeff Bridges, Alicia Keys,
Daryl Hall, Ray Bradbury, Anna Kendrick,
B. B. King, Elmore Leonard, Deepak Chopra,
AND 42 MORE CELEBRITIES
SHARE WHAT THEY'RE
MOST THANKFUL FOR

on gratitude

Sheryl Crow, Jeff Bridges, Alicia Keys,
Daryl Hall, Ray Bradbury, Anna Kendrick,
B. B. King, Elmore Leonard, Deepak Chopra,
AND 42 MORE CELEBRITIES
SHARE WHAT THEY'RE
MOST THANKFUL FOR

by TODD AARON JENSEN

Avon, Massachusetts

Published by
Adams Media, a division of F+W Media, Inc.
57 Littlefield Street, Avon, MA 02322. U.S.A.

ISBN 10: 1-4405-0594-2
ISBN 13: 978-1-4405-0594-2
eISBN 10: 1-4405-0892-5
eISBN 13: 978-1-4405-0892-9

Printed in the United States of America.

10 9 8 7 6 5 4 3 2 1

Library of Congress Cataloging-in-Publication Data
is available from the publisher.

This publication is designed to provide accurate and authoritative information with
regard to the subject matter covered. It is sold with the understanding that the publisher is not engaged in rendering legal, accounting, or other professional advice. If
legal advice or other expert assistance is required, the services of a competent professional person should be sought.
—From a *Declaration of Principles* jointly adopted by a Committee of the American Bar
Association and a Committee of Publishers and Associations

Many of the designations used by manufacturers and sellers to distinguish their
product are claimed as trademarks. Where those designations appear in this book
and Adams Media was aware of a trademark claim, the designations have been
printed with initial capital letters.

Excerpt on page 54 from the poem "When I Die" (copyright 1968 by Nikki
Giovanni) used with permission from author.

This book is available for bulk purchases. For information, please call 1-800-289-0963.

dedication

For the lovers, lunatics, and poets

That would be, in no particular or incriminating order,
My parents, my children, my bride, and—most probably—

Thank *you* . . .

cast of characters

introduction

THIRD GRADE: Mrs. Bammel, pregnant with her first child, cracks open the math book. It's time to teach negative numbers. It goes like this: You start at zero. If you move to the right of zero, you're in the positive. Simple stuff: 1, 2, 3. If you move to the left of zero, you're in . . . wait? *What?* Negative numbers. Makes no sense: -1, -2, -3 . . . . As toe-tinglingly in love as you are with Mrs. Bammel, with her Dutch-boy haircut, caramel voice, and bottomless treasure chest of glue, glitter, and felt, you have to protest. "Mrs. Bammel, excuse me, Mrs. *Bammel* . . . . Why in the world would we count negative numbers? That's counting what's *not* there!"

Mrs. Bammel makes a decent mathematical argument, though at nine years old, you're still scratching your head. Thirty years later, you are an expert in negative numbers, a master at counting what's *not* there.

You count the things you've lost—the *lack*. It goes like this: You lost your marriage, your best friend, your house, your dog, all of your grand-parents—and quickly. You lost your favorite shirt (the proverbial shirt off your back, one supposes). You've either lost money or a laundry list of dreams you had when you were a kid, maybe both, and probably a little faith, too. Your life is a veritable country-western song. And you don't even *like* country-western music. Here you are: The *becoming* has led you to *being* all the things you've always feared or hated.

You can count your lack forever, and it's easy to do, and if you're always only counting then you're always *never* at risk of losing anything ever again.

Except even when you think you've lost everything, you're never without. In fact, this is the perfect moment to allow gratitude to be your guru, to whisper with grace small words of thanks for everything—*anything*—in your life. Begin like this: I am alive.

The funny thing about life's riches, they were always there; *I* wasn't. Becoming present was not the result of therapy, or chiropractic adjustments, or yoga, or aimless road trips, though all of those things certainly helped. The real key was, simply, listening without borders, boundaries, or expectations. Letting go of the knowing and, really, just living in the experience. You are surrounded by people who are living in bliss. I was. I *am*. And it is our duty, as Kurt Vonnegut shared weeks before his passing in 2007, to help each other through this life in whatever ways we can.

As a journalist, it is my job to listen. So, discarding the third grade math lessons of Mrs. Bammel, I chose to listen. *Really* listen. And an ode to joy is what I heard, sung in the voices of our modern-day gods—superstars of the silver screen, the sports arena, the pop charts, and the printed page. Men and women who, in some cases, were born to poverty, stricken with terminal illness, saddled with sad songs and brutal stanzas, and yet not only survived, but thrived, and did so with a powerful sense of abundance. These people, they do not only thank their agents and their parents on awards shows, but many of them maintain very active gratitude lists even when the world is not looking.

What I found: Listening felt good. It felt great. I was receiving so much, by simply being more present. This was an enormous gift I was given, with each conversation, each simple parable, anecdote, testimony, or revelation. The more I listened to the gratitude of others, the more grateful I felt in my own life, and the more compelled I felt to share with others that which was given to me. You cannot read these interviews without being reminded of the great gift that is your own life, without experiencing a profound ignition of your own passions and curiosities about the world in which we live, without discovering anew or for the first time high magic and low puns and great possibilities and unexpected delights that exist right here and now in this universe. *Your* universe.

That is the intention of this book. *On Gratitude* is an invitation, first, to listen, to be moved as I have been moved, and then, more importantly, to share in turn, that together we might launch a revolution of sorts, a minor movement toward a higher consciousness that puts at a premium the simple act of counting our blessings and sharing them with others.

If we teach that which we most need to learn, then call this my path and I will walk it, and proudly. I ask that you join me. How beautiful would this world be if we counted all that we have and not what we've lost or never had? It may be that you are grateful for your library card or an old pair of overalls . . . surviving cancer or coming to America . . . the Sondheim songbook or the sojourn to Egypt . . . a fruit drink from the Philippines or your first typewriter . . . avocados or baseball. These are a few things I heard about when I began listening.

Truth is, though, your gratitude means as much as anyone else's. And so I am listening, still. We are listening. The world is listening. Wherever you are, let it begin now, like this:

I am grateful for . . .

—Todd Aaron Jensen

todd@thegratitudelist.org, www.thegratitudelist.org

Kristen Bell

on gratitude

"I'm grateful that my mother knew what to do with a tiny tomboy who wanted everyone to call her Smurfette when she was three years old."

KRISTEN BELL is one of Hollywood's most talented ingénues, a flaxen-haired actress with a spritely, spunky aura, a machine-gun wit, and a diverse career that alternates turns on Broadway, genre TV gigs, and big screen romantic comedies. Oh, and she's also impossibly hot. (Just ask PETA, who has twice named her their Sexiest Vegetarian of the Year—or *Maxim*, if you must.) But there's more to Bell than that. *A lot* more. And here's her secret: She's a total geek, a dork, a nerd. She eats dessert after every meal. She loves her dogs as much as people. She gets hot and bothered about show tunes. She obsesses over the nuances and plot points of her favorite TV shows and books. She knows the difference between a DS Lite and a PS3. And she can speak a little Klingon, which just might make Kristen Bell the perfect woman. Born and raised in a suburb outside of Detroit, Bell was a tomboy with stars in her eyes, petitioning to change her name to Smurfette when she was but a toddler, already starring in school plays and doing regional modeling work by the age of eleven. One can imagine calendar pages flying, montage-like, through the air as teenaged Bell sang and danced the Great White Way's most famous show tunes to her bedroom mirror, Stephen Sondheim's being her favorites. By the age of twenty-one, after a stint at NYU's Tisch School of the Arts, Bell was performing on Broadway, playing Becky Thatcher in an opulent, musical version of *Tom Sawyer*, before appearing opposite Liam Neeson and Laura Linney in Arthur Miller's *The Crucible*. For street cred, and because, after all, she is an admitted total geek, Bell quickly darted off-Broadway to breathe life into *Reefer Madness: The Musical*. Then came *Veronica Mars*, the TV cult hit about a perky detective-in-training, which made Bell a household name, followed by big-screen work in *Forgetting Sarah Marshall* and *Couples Retreat*. These career accomplishments fail to reveal the other "secrets" Bell possesses, the things that lend her an air of gravity, a quote-unquote realness that provides depth to the pristine surface: the tragedy that struck her life at sixteen, the months she served the underprivileged of Brazil, and her great glee at being tackled by "giant, hairy men" every time she comes home (for the record, she means her dogs). Survey says, we've not begun to scratch the surface of all that Bell has to offer, as she tolls for you—and fanboys everywhere around the world. Nerdy may be the new cool, as she is wont to say, but thanks to Kristen Bell, it's also never been hotter.

WHISTLE A HAPPY TUNE. My mother heard me humming around the house when I was a child. Since I was too small to play sports and was also not very coordinated, she put me in singing lessons, and I started competing in solo and ensemble competitions when I was about thirteen. To this day, music is very, very important to me. Music got me to musical theater, got me to acting, which got me to this career I'm having. I'm grateful that my mother knew what to do with a tiny tomboy who wanted everyone to call her Smurfette when she was three years old.

"GREEN FINCH AND LINNET BIRD." When I heard it, it was one of the first times I cared not only about the notes in a song, but the character in a song. Stephen Sondheim's music is so unexpected. His chords are so often dissonant. The harmonies are surprising to the ear. It's complex. It's very, very layered. Lyrically, his perspectives—especially when he's writing women—are almost completely unique. He doesn't write the typical, "Woe is me; I'm in love." He *really* does it for me.

KRISTEN BELL SAVES THE UNIVERSE. I went to Brazil when I was nineteen, and I came back a completely different person. I was on a volunteer mission and worked at an orphanage in Bel Horizonte for about a month and a half. I was basically exposed to a lifestyle that was polar opposite to the one I grew up with—kids with no homes, who are basically running down the streets away from the cops; who had no education, no drive, no hope. Struggling to round them up was a task in and of itself for these missionaries and volunteers. Some of the kids just didn't want help and that was really powerful. How do you cry a tear for someone who doesn't want what they might need? That gives you a lot of perspective at a time when most of us really need it.

KRISTEN BELL, OBSTETRICIAN. While I was Brazil, I was also asked to help out around the hospital. This hospital was absolutely barren. They didn't even have enough rubber gloves, and they disposed of their "sharps" in a two-liter soda bottle. Not everyone had masks in the operating rooms. There just wasn't enough to go around. It was very eye-opening. I assisted on minor surgeries, acted as a triage nurse. Two of the days that I was working there, women showed up and said, "I'm ready to pop. Let's do this!" So I helped some babies be born. It was unbelievable.

SORROW FLOATS. I had a fairly easy childhood. Sure, my parents were divorced when I was little, and they remarried and had more kids, but really I just ended up with lots more people who love me. To feel your mortality at sixteen is very scary, which is what happened to me when my best friend died in a car accident. It was horrible, unexpected, but it also really changed my life in surprising ways. I came to see that without yin there is no yang. When you feel a loss that deeply, the next time you open your eyes, you see a different world.

AN ACTOR'S LIFE FOR ME. No one's forced into the acting world. No one's parents say, "You have to be an actor!" This is a career people choose because they love it. Yeah, the hours are long, but, ultimately, you're doing something creative and something you love to do. I am fully aware of this career's mortality, that it could all be taken away at any moment. So I'm grateful for every single little thing.

THE FORCE IS WITH HER. The funny thing is: I was never out to become a genre actress or to pick super-cool fanboy projects. I was just looking for good writing and interesting characters. But the people who write this stuff (*Veronica Mars*, *Heroes*, *Forgetting Sarah Marshall*) and who love this stuff are some of the most fascinating, passionate people we have. If you can keep up with the plotline of *Star Trek* for ten years and then hop onto the new generation, then you're no joke. If you take the time to learn to speak Klingon, you're in a school all your own. You obviously have a lot of brain power that the rest of us don't have. I'm very grateful that I've been allowed into that world and embraced by fans like that. It has separated me, in a lot of ways, from a lot of the girls I might otherwise get lumped in with. I will forever worship the fanboys for allowing me to feel special in that way.

Ray Bradbury
on gratitude

*"Love is the answer
to everything.
It's the only reason
to do anything."*

IF A PROPHET LIVES LONG ENOUGH, he'll see the future become the past. So it's been for Ray Bradbury who, now ninety, has probably seen it all, and told the tale—book-burning firemen, metaphysical carnivals, Martian conflicts, wall-sized televisions, fascism in America, and iPods, too—in classic works like *Fahrenheit 451*, *The Martian Chronicles*, *The Illustrated Man*, *Dandelion Wine*, and the recent short story collection *The Stuff That Dreams Are Made Of*. Unlike many science fiction writers, octogenarians themselves or dearly departed, Bradbury has never been a Cassandra of bleak overtures. Nor is he a hardware junkie. Rather, for sixty years, Bradbury has been a forecaster of sunny skies, or even odds anyway. His work is Romantic, chivalric, steeped in feverish, childlike reverie and fantasy. "I am a child who never grew up," Bradbury proudly professes, his finger thrust declaratively into the air. "And I'm proud of

THE MOTHER OF INVENTION. I was thirty years old. I had a house with a baby in it, making loud noises. I needed an office but couldn't afford one. I was up at UCLA one day and I heard typing coming from down below in the library basement. I went down and looked and saw that there were typewriters for rent, ten cents for half an hour. I got a big bag of dimes and moved into this typing room at UCLA, and I spent $9.80 over nine days and I wrote *Fahrenheit 451*. Cost me $9.80.

WHAT DREAMS ARE MADE OF. Love is easy. You can't resist love. You get an idea, someone says something, and you're in love. I went to dinner in Denver about twenty years ago and heard the lady at the next table say to her friends, "Oh, my God, I'll bet dogs think every day is Christmas." I went up to her and said, "Madam, thank you. You've just given me a title. I'm going back to my hotel, and I'm going to write a book called *Dogs Think That Every Day Is Christmas*." That's how these things happen.

THE SECRET O' LIFE. You just do it, that's how. Its pure Zen Buddhism: *Don't try to do, just do.* Do what you love and love what you do. That's the basic rule of life. If you live this life without trying, it's good. If you try too hard, it won't be any good. It just has to be done, period—like an explosion.

THE PERFECT 10. Bo Derek came into my life twenty-five years ago. I was in a train station in France, and this pretty girl came up to me and said, "Mr. Bradbury?" I said, "Yes?" She said, "I love you." I said, "Who are you?" She said, "My name is Bo Derek." I said, "Oh my God. Is it really?" She said, "Yes, it is, Mr. Bradbury. Will you ride on the train with me?" I said, "*Whooooooaaaa*! Okay, yeah!" So I rode on the train with her. I was with her for two days. Can you imagine what that was like, to be with Bo Derek for two days when she was at the peak of her fame and popularity and beauty? Every hour on the hour, she came up to me and hugged me and kissed me and said, "Ray, I love you." What more does a man need? Last August, she came to my birthday party, and the same thing happened all over again. She put her arms around me and said, "Ray, I still love you."

LIFE ON MARS. I insist they bury me on Mars. When I die, I want them to take my ashes. I want to be the first dead person on Mars—not the first live one, but the first dead one.

Jeff Bridges
on gratitude

*"When you truly commit in your
life, you start receiving more than
you could imagine."*

THAT DUSKY OPTIMISM, that wounded twilight, the fear or passion or yearning, and almost always in the name of good—that's what Oscar-winner Jeff Bridges wears on his face, sometimes draped from that sneaky, sardonic grin, sometimes hooked on those twinkling, wizened eyes. There is mischief afoot behind that visage, and hunger, too, and a wisdom hard-earned from a lifetime of playing killers and cowboys, lovers and dreamers, everymen survivors and fractured spirits. You watch Bridges's face onscreen in, say, *Fearless* or *The Fisher King*, *The Big Lebowski* or *American Heart*, *The Last Picture Show* or *Crazy Heart* (for which he finally won the Oscar in 2010), and you bear witness to the kind of weary intelligence and unblinking emotion a man, who is going in grace, wears in the final moments before the floor drops out beneath him. You also see the work of an American actor about as great as any who has ever lived. Like many of the characters Bridges has portrayed, the actor's career has occasionally been rambling, reckless, and unpredictable—prototypically American, in other words. There appears to be no rhyme or reason to the creative choices of Jeff Bridges, no major concessions to Tinseltown tomfoolery or massive paydays. (Indeed, Bridges turned down such "sure things" as *Speed*, *48 Hours*, *Big*, and *Raiders of the Lost Ark*). Instead, what audiences have enjoyed is a genuine artist at work, a creative spirit following his bliss. If human beings are possessed of an "inner voice," then surely this is the siren to which Bridges has long steered his ship. But Bridges is also one of us. While Pacino and Hoffman and DeNiro, Bridges's immediate contemporaries, are larger than life and frequently histrionic, Bridges is a god who walks entirely among us, in our attire, on our streets, and with our faces. "When I come away from a movie, there's an appreciation of having been through a little lifetime in someone else's skin," Bridges says. "There are things you never want to forget." When we spoke, Bridges was an affable, radiant host, laid-back, completely comfortable in his own skin, eager to invite a guest to the endless buffet of good fortune and great times that makes up his life. If we were one day asked to play Jeff Bridges, to live a little lifetime in *his* skin, these are the gifts he would ask of us.

APRON STRINGS. When my siblings and I were growing up, my mother, Dorothy, gave us what she called "Time"—one hour every day, without fail, to do whatever we wanted with her. She didn't answer the phone, wouldn't answer the door. She'd just spend an hour with me, totally, every day, even into my twenties. "What do you want to do with your Time, Jeff?" "How about a massage, Mom?" And she'd rub me for an hour. Or, when I was a kid, "Let's go into your makeup, Mom. I want to make you up like a clown!" "Let's play spaceship, and you're the alien!" That was one of her mothering tools, and I certainly felt loved.

FATHER TO SON. If my father (actor Lloyd Bridges) was a shoemaker, I probably would have been a shoemaker. I learned how to act from my father, but, more important than that, I learned how to *behave* from my father. I think that's brought a lot of good stuff into my life, just behaving well, like my father did.

GIVE AND TAKE. Moviemaking is a collaborative art form. Ninety percent of your success comes from who you play with. You bring all your stuff to the table, but you have to remain open to the impulses and ideas of other people. That's where the rich stuff comes from. Not just in making movies, but in life, too.

TOLTEC WISDOM. I got a lot out of this wonderful book, *The Four Agreements*. I love the section on being impeccable with your word. Words are almost like spells; they're *that* powerful—not only the words you say to other people, but the words you say to yourself. You can't take yourself too seriously, and you can't take your thoughts too seriously. They're only thoughts. That awareness allows what you really are to just be there, to be open. I believe that's where creativity and happiness come from.

HERO OF 1,000 FACES. It can be really lucrative to do one thing over and over, but I saw the suffering typecasting caused my dad. He was so successful on *Sea Hawk* that people actually thought he was a skin diver. Then he was so good in the *Airplane* movies that people thought he could only do comedy. It's a great compliment to his talent, but it also really limited the jobs he was offered. I thought if I just happily confused the audience each time out, gave them a scattering of different kinds of roles through the years, then they might never have me pegged or figured out. They could just appreciate who I was in that moment. Maybe it's worked.

I AM, I SAID. After about ten movies and an Oscar nomination, I still wasn't sure I really wanted to be an actor. This is back in the early '70s. I just wouldn't commit. So I finished this movie, *The Last American Hero*, and I didn't want to work, but I got a call saying John Frankenheimer wanted to cast me in *The Iceman Cometh* with Lee Marvin, Robert Ryan, and Frederic March. I passed. "Ah, I'm bushed. No thanks," whatever.

Five minutes later, the director of *The Last American Hero* called me up and said, "You call yourself an actor. You're no actor. I'm never talking to you again." And he hung up on me. I thought, "Gee, let's think about this for a second. Am I an actor or not?" You know, being a professional means you have to work sometimes, even when you don't feel like it. But I decided then and there that, yes, I'm an actor. I took that movie. We rehearsed for eight weeks, shot in two, and I can't tell you how much I learned about acting from being around these legends, these old acting masters, like Robert Ryan and Lee Marvin. When you truly commit in your life, you start receiving more than you could imagine. That's how it's worked for me.

THE JUDO OF I DO. My wife is the big blessing in my life. We've been married more than thirty years. Marriage is a funny judo deal— the so-called obstacles and pitfalls, the tough stuff, those are the real blessings. The fun stuff can be the real trap. You have to appreciate the obstacles as opportunities to open up more than you thought you could, connect more deeply than you thought you could. Nothing is too big for you when you're really *with* your partner, like my wife and I are together.

THE MAGIC CUE BALL. Get rid of your hair, like I did for *Iron Man.* I've got to tell you, it was a really liberating experience. Shave your head. You really get to know your face, what it's made of, and that's a real blessing. The first couple days of growth afterward are kind of scratchy. Your head's got teeth. But then four days go by and you get the "teddy bear nose"—it's like velvet. But get rid of your hair and see who you are.

Alton Brown
on gratitude

"Hospitality is all about graciously giving and taking. It's simply sharing what you have and taking what is offered."

YOU CAN WILE AWAY A LIFETIME tilting at windmills, dreaming impossible dreams, watching others get free passes for mediocrity, or you can get off your motorcycle, lay down your Panavision movie camera, walk away from REM, enroll yourself in a prestigious cooking school, and become the best-known on-camera chef this side of Julia Child and Emeril Lagasse. For Alton Brown, who has dominated Food Network's broadcast schedule for most of a decade with shows like *Good Eats* and *Iron Chef America,* the choice was simple. An avid biker and aspiring filmmaker (who shot REM's breakout music video, "The One I Love," way back in the 1980s), Brown found himself vaguely dissatisfied with his day job, shooting infomercials for General Electric and music videos for up-and-coming bands. Instead, his attention was always pulled to shows about cooking, which, he believed, sucked. Intent on producing a masterpiece, and remembering that "chicks dig a guy who can cook," Brown made his way to the renowned New England Culinary Institute, where he naturally excelled, though his scientific approach frequently irked his professors. Three years after graduation, in 1999, Food Network debuted Brown's D.I.Y. cooking extravaganza, *Good Eats*. A sizzling combination of wit, wisdom, science, pop culture, and, yes, food, *Eats* is more than soups and soufflés. It's almost pop art with zucchini as a guest star—a dizzying series of food-based science experiments, puns, Monty Python-style tomfoolery, recipes, and basement antics, all anchored by Brown's irresistible, deadpan persona. *Good Eats*, currently enjoying its eleventh year on air, has been a gravy train for Brown, spawning spinoff shows on Food Network and bestselling books. In 2007, *Good Eats* claimed a Peabody Award, honoring excellence in broadcast news, education, and entertainment. Today, Brown is a household name, assuming you spend any time with skillets or bok choy, and he has no trouble filling his plate with gratitude.

MEDIUMS WELL. There are so many forms of communication and community available to us today, and so many opportunities for what I call "creative transfer." I'm grateful for any opportunity to work in a new arena or medium, as long as I don't have to contradict my "career DNA." I did an *Iron Chef* video game a couple of years ago, and it was amazing—like being a part of "the new storytelling." Any chance to connect with people today in a positive way is something to be grateful for.

THE SCIENCE OF SERENDIPITY. I went to New England Culinary Institute to get the background I needed to start making shows about food. I knew when I got there that I wanted to deal with know-how rather than recipes, but it took me discovering that I have no natural talents as a chef to really go out and seek science as an answer to my questions. What's odd is that I flunked science classes in high school and college and now I get invitations to teach. Weird.

THINKING LIKE MACGYVER. I'm just a guy who thinks like a guy—which means I like to solve problems with whatever I have around.

If I can concoct a new angle on a solution, even better. But man, Mac-Gyver's hair . . . I don't have that hair.

ELBOW GREASE. I have no idea where creativity comes from. If I did, I'd go there and beg for it on a regular basis. I can tell you this, though, creativity doesn't bless the idle. You have to work. Work and the creativity will come . . . if it feels like it. If it doesn't, well, at least there's work.

AMBER WAVES OF GRAIN. There are two "best" ways to see the country: from the back of a bike and from an airplane flying low and slow (I'm a licensed pilot). They're opposite sides of the same beautiful coin. Motorcycles allow full immersion and an almost infinite ability to improvise. From the air, you get to see the true patterns of life. It's a subtle difference really.

CHERRY ON TOP. I won't lie; accolades are sweet. I have been blessed with three real beauties: a James Beard award, the Bon Appétit teaching award, and the Peabody. All amazing, but I have to tell you, as a filmmaker, the Peabody is the pinnacle. And to be the only food person since Julia Child to get one is just insane.

MI CASA ES SU CASA. Hospitality is all about graciously giving and taking. It's not about impressing people or overwhelming them with your cleverness or skill. It's simply sharing what you have and taking what is offered. The greatest hospitality I've ever been shown is when I invited someone to my house for dinner without knowing they were vegetarian. They ate the food that was offered with nothing but a heartfelt "thank you." And baby, it was ribs.

Deepak Chopra
on gratitude

"If you can help without any need for recognition, that is actually, truly a spiritual lifetime. It is nice to do things without the need for ego gratification."

YOU'VE PROBABLY HEARD: Laughter is the best medicine. And so these days, Dr. Deepak Chopra tells a lot of jokes. Delivered in his preternaturally tranquil voice, a heavily accented instrument, these ha-has are all part of the good doctor's prescription for a better, happier life. If it surprises you that the gags of Chopra—a spiritual guru, international bestseller, and "the poet-prophet of alternative medicine," according to *Time Magazine*—occasionally veer to the risqué, that's exactly the point. "The measure of your enlightenment is the degree to which you're comfortable with paradox, contradiction, and ambiguity," he says, referencing an ancient Indian maxim. "So, when I tell a joke about an old man and a young woman in hell, the punch line is not what you expect. You are laughing, but, also, it helps you shift your perspective a little bit. This is a step to enlightenment." Chopra's own road to enlightenment began six decades ago in Srinagar, India. As a child, Chopra was caught in the crossfire between a father who was a very traditional—and very success-ful—cardiologist and a grandfather who favored Ayurvedic medicine, an alternative means of healing. The young Chopra loved both, studied both, and has spent a storied, richly rewarded career offering his own "ultimate happiness prescription," a combination of hard science, positive psychology, and Eastern spirituality. Having sold more than 20 million books and operating the Chopra Center for Well-Being, he has become a poster boy for the New Age movement, sharing his wisdom through his writing and an extremely active international lecture schedule. But with all things, too, he keeps a sense of levity. "It is balance," Chopra says. In comedian Mike Myers's second chakra mantra-and-pooh fest, 2008's *The Love Guru*, Chopra playfully skewers his own image, allowing Myers—in full Peter Sellers mode—to lampoon the spirituality movement. Along the way, even with a sense of humor and detachment cultivated by decades of meditation and yoga, Chopra has also become a lightning rod for naysayers and skeptics who care not for his "don't worry, be happy" answers to questions that are more profitably answered by pharmacy vis-its. "It takes discipline and commitment to meditate every day, but noth-ing to criticize," Chopra says, with all the fuss of a grocery-list recitation. Crowned one of the twentieth century's top 100 heroes and icons by *Time* in 1999, Chopra believes the gap between traditional medicine and more progressive healing methods is rapidly closing. From his viewpoint, the things we *know* and the things we've only been able to *believe* are rapidly becoming one in the same; how we live really *does* affect how we feel; a more complete mind-body connection, along with healing and prosperity are available to us all now. And that's no joke.

THE RECREATIONAL UNIVERSE. We've made life a battlefield when it should be a playground. It's all about beauty, wonder, mystery . . . but we forget that, and almost purposefully. We must have a more mindful attitude. Be mindful of your breath. Be mindful of your body sensations. Be mindful of your choices. These are good ways to actually know your experiences, to remember to play and be alive.

FREE AT LAST. I do not need to catch my breath today. I do not know stress any longer.

TURNING A PAGE. The underlying theme in Sinclair Lewis's *Arrowsmith* is the quest for awakening, more than anything else, and it includes the theme of healing, too. It's about somebody who accidentally kills someone else and then, later becomes an anonymous doer of good deeds. He helps people anonymously, etcetera, etcetera. This was inspiring to me as a young man. If you can help without any need for recognition, that is actually, truly a spiritual lifetime. It is nice to do things without the need for ego gratification.

DISCOVERING OM. I was in a hotel in Washington D.C., a med student, young and curious, coming out of the restroom and Maharishi Mahesh Yogi (the founder of Transcendental Meditation) was in the lobby of the hotel, and he spotted me and said, "You! Come to my room." That was it. I was an Indian in Washington D.C., and so was he. That's all either one of us knew, though we both knew it was an intuition and a blessing that we should meet. I studied meditation with him for twelve years from that night forward. It changed my life entirely. If I had not needed to use the restroom in that five minute span, my life would have been different.

THE SUFI POET OF LOVE. Rumi speaks of divine ecstasy through love—both human love and divine love. This is ecstatic. It can shift your consciousness. It can lead you to exuberance and exultation. It can elevate your spirit. And, as you are finding your love, there is always the poetry of Rumi. You *must* read this.

THE FACTS OF LIFE. I have been married for forty years. The secret? Total acceptance and give up being right. It's the advice for everyone in every relationship. You will be grateful for this advice, whether it is in your marriage or your parenting, your brotherhood, or your business.

NEVER HUNGRY, ALWAYS FULL. I grew up in India, so one of my favorite foods growing up was always fish curry. But, basically, I'm grateful for every meal that I have, whatever it is. I eat when I'm hungry, not to satisfy any other kind of hunger.

REINVENTING THE BODY, RESURRECTING THE SOUL. There is wonderful research going on right now about neuroplasticity (or cortical remapping), how we can actually change the structure of our brains. There is also great research about the fact that our mutated genes—from Huntington's to polio to cystic fibrosis, along with things like obesity and cancers and other illnesses—can be remedied, repaired, redirected. You can actually turn off the bad genes, while keeping the good ones active. These things are affected by the way you think, by your personal relationships, by exercise, yoga, and diet, stress management. This is very interesting information. You have 100 trillion cells in your body, which is more than all of the stars in the Milky Way galaxy, and they are regulated by these nanocomputers in every cell called genes. And you can change them. If you can change your genes and you can change the structure of your brain, then you can change your whole body. This is something to be grateful for.

PEAS IN A POD. If something is real, then you shouldn't have to rely on belief or faith. Belief is a cover-up for insecurity. The most fervent believers, of course, are fundamentalists, and they're making a bit of a mess of the world. If I ask you, "Do you believe in gravity or electricity?" you'd say, "What kind of a question is that?" Similarly, if you have a soul or if God exists, belief is not the way to have that experience. There should simply be clarity. You should know, scientifically and experientially speaking, and the belief follows that. These are not things to cling to, but to embrace.

GRACE IS ... Some divine intelligence that leads us in the right direction.

GOOD MORNING, SUNSHINE. I wake up every day with a sense of gratitude and a sense of newness. Every day is a new day for me. I don't really spend time anticipating, and I'm not victimized by memories, so it's fun to be alive. You should try it.

Francis Ford Coppola
on gratitude

"This is my talent: I can come up with a creative solution to any problem. But that's not genius. Mozart—that's genius."

FOR ALL THAT HE HAS LOVED AND LOST—including multiple fortunes, a decade-long run in the 1970s as the world's greatest filmmaker and, most devastatingly, the accidental death of his son, Gio, in 1986—the world keeps making Francis Ford Coppola offers he cannot refuse. But heartbreak has no room to blossom in the curious man, and neither does stagnation. Even in his seventies, Coppola engages with the world as a child of wonder, not only marching to the beat of his own drum, but *being* the drum, too. There is music in Coppola, even if the rest of us don't always hear it, and it is operatic—the lush, symphonic score to a life story full of exploration, indulgence, and sheer brilliance. The man who won five Oscars of his own (for his work on *The Godfather*, *The Godfather II*, and the screenplay for *Patton*) and directed twelve actors to Oscar-nominated performances began his life, though, a sickly child, bed-ridden with polio. A quarantined ten-year old, the young Coppola retreated into his imagination, making up stories based on old Italian folklore and ancient fairy tales, coupling them with the crude technology available to him: handmade puppets, a reel-to-reel tape recorder, and a Super-8 movie camera. His sick bed was a Plato's cave of sorts, but also a film school. Coppola has always been a master of the D.I.Y. ethos, insatiable in his curiosity and unstoppable in his drive—which is why a film like *Apocalypse Now* took years to make, drove countless cast and crew members to nervous breakdowns, and nearly took the life of star Martin Sheen. After fifteen years of yeomanlike studio work in the '80s and '90s, Coppola rebounded with a diverse palette of extra-Hollywood endeavors; today he does remarkably well as a vintner, specialty food maker, magazine publisher, and owner of resorts in Belize and Guatemala. These efforts have allowed him to return to the level of personal, self-funded filmmaking he enjoyed during his days of independence and innovation in the 1960s, something for which he is deeply grateful. (Check out the recent *Youth Without Youth* and *Tetro*, if you doubt.) Today, Coppola is cloaked all in black, a beret tilted just so to the left, in his lap a plate of Tahini-based Halva, a dense and crumbly confection. He is perfectly willing to share.

THE MISSION. I only want to make deeply personal films at this point. It's so hard to make a film; you might as well make a film that asks questions you want to know the answers to. If not, what are you doing it for?

KINGS OF THE Bs. Roger Corman gave me my start in the pictures (with 1963's bargain-horror *Dementia 13*). He was a very practical guy. He was an engineer. You didn't train with him. He wisely knew that if you want to make low-budget films, you hire film students who will work for nothing except the chance to learn. Most of Roger's motives basically had to do with making money, but if you were lucky enough to work for him, he would throw you into the field at such a bottom-basement level of filmmaking that you had to sink or swim. You got to be around all that equipment and opportunity and (had to) figure out what you could do. That *worked* for me.

GOING FROM THE GUT. The artist will never know for sure if what he's doing is any good, but he has to follow his most honest instincts anyway. I don't think I ever made a movie just to make money. If I did, I'm sure it would fail. So I'm left with my instincts. If you really want to make money, there are so many better ways to do it, as I've demonstrated. It's probably better to make money with our day jobs and then go make the movies we really believe in. I think that would make better movies.

AHEAD OF THE CURVE. At this point in my career, now that I'm older, I don't want to make movies just to make movies, or just to be in the business. I want to try to make movies that are like literature, or that are like the movies I saw when I was younger—the movies that made me want to make films, the ones that inspired me, the ones that made me say, "I've never seen *that* before." So many films you see today, it's all so familiar—the kid is kidnapped, the man is haunted, the wife is anguished. It's all just formula designed to please the audience and make a lot of dough. But *sometimes* you don't please the audience and make a lot of dough, even when you're doing that kind of film. So you might as well make a film that means something to you.

THY AIM IS TRUE. I would think most artists have some ideas or arrows in the quiver and once they've shot those arrows, they may have done everything they have to do. There are giants like Shakespeare or Verdi or Kurosawa who seem to have an endless supply of ideas and inspiration—arrows. Some artists, too, become more known in their fifties, but I think it's the same idea: The arrows are just recognized later in the life. I wonder if you can go back in time and reinvent yourself by adopting a very youthful point of view? That's what I'm trying to do now. Will I ever make another *Apocalypse Now*? I hope not. And I'll keep trying.

STRANGE BREW. I was fired for writing the opening of *Patton*, which won an Oscar and is considered one of the best openings of any film. I took so much flak for *Apocalypse Now* being too different. When things are different, they rub against the grain, and they irritate, and they threaten some people. I try to make movies the same way I cook for people. I never cooked a meal thinking, "Whether they like it or not, that's the meal I'm giving them." I've never made a meal full of stuff I knew people would hate. I care. I might say, I tried to make a movie people might enjoy and if they go back to it they might find there's even more waiting for them. That's a privilege to me, that.

TO THINE OWN SELF BE TRUE. The best thing I can hope for now is some artistic fulfillment for myself, and I definitely feel pleased with where I'm at now. I'm making films now that delve into thoughts and feelings I have had about my life, and that's a real gift. Let's face it, we're all inspired by certain people when we begin. I'd love to be held in the same regard as Fellini or Tennessee Williams or Kurosawa. It's hard to be in that league, but the fact is that I'm trying as hard as I can to reach for it. Even if I fail, I've tried, and I'm okay with that. It's a mistake to lack ambition. People will often call you pretentious. *Who does he think he is?* The truth is, I don't know who I am, but I would like to be as good as the best.

GENIUS. I never felt I had the talent that I wished to have. I think what I mean to say is, I have good imagination, a lot of energy, and I'm very enthusiastic, and that's probably made up for that God-given talent that some people have to, whatever, draw beautiful pictures or compose a symphony or write poetry or dance. I've done it the hard way. I've kept trying with everything I've got. This is my talent: I can come up with a creative solution to any problem. But that's not genius. Mozart—*that's* genius. I don't have that.

AND IN THE END. Here's the story: This young guy becomes a famous moviemaker, he buys a movie studio, he loses all his money. That's a good opening to become Phil Spector or something. But then to say, he goes off to Napa and makes a bigger fortune in the wine business, that is unusual. Then he uses that to go back and make movies again! That's a good story. It's nice to have your life be a good story.

Sheryl Crow
on gratitude

"To find a lyric that comes together to teach me about myself is a real blessing."

THE FIRST TIME WE HEARD Sheryl Crow's voice (on "Run Baby Run," the lead track of her debut album, 1993's *Tuesday Night Music Club*), she was a world-weary, spiritual fugitive, all grownup but all run down. She seemed stuck between Kansas and Oz and dizzy without a map, her lyrics penned in tears, instruments soaked in whiskey. Any light provided, perhaps, came from a broken window and a heavy sun. Fifteen years later, Crow closed her *Detours* album with the gentle affirmation, "love is all there is." It's not that life between "Leaving Las Vegas" and "Lullaby for Wyatt" has gotten any simpler for Crow. Indeed, in recent years, she has successfully battled breast cancer, endured a high-profile breakup with cycling superstar Lance Armstrong, and become a new parent to two sons, Wyatt and Levi. No, life's the same—old, same-old of trials and tribulations; it's *Crow* that's different, living more mindfully, meditatively, and with more gratitude. In other words, it's the singer, stupid, not the song. The first chapters of Crow's life were lessons in fat chance, good fortune, and hard luck, if you believe in that kind of thing. She grew up a big fish in a little Missouri pond, popular in school and well loved at home, raised in a musical family with a solid spiritual foundation. After college, Crow stayed close to home and taught music to elementary school children, gigging in roots rock and cover bands on the weekends, eventually picking up some five-figure paychecks laying down hot licks on radio commercial jingles. A couple of those, and she packed up the truck for Los Angeles, landing plum gigs singing backup vocals for Michael Jackson and Don Henley. Contracts and ink promptly followed, but Crow's debut album was a long time coming; it was forged with blood, sweat, tears, and a trail of broken relationships and collaborations. Nevertheless, the release of *Tuesday Night Music Club*, and its subsequent, stratospheric commercial and critical impact, made Crow an overnight success—a decade after her first professional gig. Songs like "Strong Enough," "All I Wanna Do," and "Leaving Las Vegas" immediately announced the arrival of a formidable talent, capable of balancing buoyant, tipsy rock and bluesy, wizened balladry with a penchant for freestyle wordplay and an attuned ear for hooks and melodies. Six additional studio albums have firmly established Crow as one of rock's essential female performers. Over the years, she has sold 25 million albums, picked up nine Grammy Awards, found her grace and peace through difficult times in meditation, friendship, and parenthood. As she once sang, "a change would do you good." Truer words were rarely sung, and it's advice beautifully heeded by the singer herself.

RUNNER'S HIGH. I used to jog every day, and I'd call it my "gratitude run." I'd make my gratitude list as I ran. I never ran out of things to be grateful for. My knees aren't what they used to be, but I still do my gratitude list every day.

LEARNING HOW TO CRAWL. I grew up in a church, and I've always been around people who taught me to pray. I've always spent my days praying and being grateful. It's always been a part of my spiritual makeup, that strong consciousness that God is always with me. It began with my parents, my mom especially, who are spiritual seekers. I've had other great teachers along the way. It's important to be reminded of what's important.

THIRD EYE KIND. Mindfulness meditation is something I practice. The idea of it is to clear your mind. When you're distracted, and the mind won't stop, you don't beat yourself up; you show yourself compassion and you suddenly become awake, but clearer. That's a nice way to treat yourself.

LIVING THE DREAM. The moments where I've had those awesome moments of "wow, I'm really doing what I'm supposed to be doing" is when I've been playing overseas in places I never dreamed of going or being, playing music I really love. Every once in a while, I'll be on a stage in some distant corner of the world, and I'll have that sort of moment of awakening where I feel extremely humbled to do what I'm doing. The thought is, "I never could have dreamed I'd be here, ever—forget that I'd be here like *this*." It's humbling.

CLOSER TO GOD. I always say that writing, for me, is like going to church. When I'm out of my own way, when my ego is hushed, when my propensity for judging myself and editing myself is silenced for a moment, I'm feeling pretty close to God and everything's good. To find a lyric that comes together to teach me about myself is a real blessing. I wrote a lot of my last record (*Detours*) at six in the morning, right after feeding my baby, really enjoying the quiet and appreciating the thoughts that come at that hour.

THIS MAMA SAYS. I think that spirits pick their parents in some way, shape, or form. I cannot say how humbling it is to be chosen like that. And I'm deeply grateful that I have the family that I have to help me raise him.

SAMSARA SHRUGGED. Your life can be perfect or it can be a mess, but the lessons are always there, and the truth is: There will always be bumps. The question is: When you get past the bumps, how much did you learn, how much wisdom did you gain? For me, "going through it" is where the lessons are learned. I know that with breast cancer, the lesson for me was about working with the emotions—the being scared and being sad. We Westerners usually bury all of our emotions by staying busy or distracted, so we end up holding all of these feelings—but deeply and covered up. When we're going through pain, we get busier, a lot of us, and I think that works against us. Emotion is where we really experience our awakening. For me, going through cancer was about learning how to really experience it—instead of pushing it way deep down inside and not dealing with it. By learning how to do that, I experienced it, but when I was done with it, I was really done with it. Being present in the experience is so important.

PATRIOTISM. I feel extremely lucky that I was born in this country. Even though we're going through really, really rugged times, and seem to have really fallen asleep in a lot of ways, I still believe America is an incredibly special place to live.

Roger Ebert
on gratitude

"Just do the next right thing, and be grateful for the chance you have to go do that."

THE POWER OF THE WRITTEN WORD was never made more clear to him than the moment Roger Ebert was told he would not speak again (the result of complications stemming from his decade-long battle with thyroid cancer). Ebert may not speak again, as doctors insisted, but the world would not lose the Pulitzer Prize-winning journalist's voice. *That* would always survive, and so, too, would his pointing thumbs, which became a simple and graphic scale to weigh, praise, or even sentence films to death. (Arguably, Ebert has the most famous thumbs of all time, next to Jack Kerouac and, maybe, the Fonz.) It's impossible to imagine film criticism without him: film critic for the *Chicago Sun-Times* since 1967, host of *At the Movies* and other televised movie review shows for some thirty years (most famously with Gene Siskel), author of several bestselling books about film, and founder of the annual Roger Ebert Film Festival. It's probable that more people would recognize Roger Ebert, a newspaper guy who happened to be on television once a week, giving a thumbs up or down to a handful of movies, than would know the visages of James Cameron, Michael Bay, or Steven Spielberg. And Ebert did it all honestly, without the slightest bit of sensation, scandal, chest-thumping, or self-aggrandizement. If Pauline Kael, the *other* world-famous film critic, lost it at the movies, Ebert found it, brushed it off, and returned it to the world better than before. (It's true; many of Ebert's film reviews are smarter and more entertaining than the films they assay.) Ebert became popular without ever being condescending; he found celebrity without ever courting attention, and, most importantly, advocated for the art and artists he admired genuinely and passionately. It's unlikely that any aspiring filmmaker ever picked up a camera hoping Ebert would one day review his masterpiece, but Ebert's powerful patronage (by way of the global reach of his byline and his indie-centric film festival) has certainly been a gift horse for countless young filmmakers. He is, according to *Forbes*, "the most powerful pundit in America." Perhaps the key to Ebert's longevity, and the trust we have instilled in him as our national critic, lies in this simple fact: He does it all with love. Ebert has never been a nihilist, a destroyer, or muckraker, or an Old Testament eye-gouger, not even in recent years when his health has conspired against him. No, Ebert writes about film because he truly, wholeheartedly loves cinema, and he greets each new film as if it could be a new, beloved cousin on the great family tree of movie masterpieces; he heralds the birth and sings it into being. In a day where entertainment reporting is demolition derby and Gospel truth all at once, Ebert is our last great hope—a gentleman and a scholar. It's no surprise that he lives a life of gratitude and counts his blessings daily, the lists routinely outnumbering the thumbs he has, and the words, too, probably.

THE ZOETROPE OF LIFE. We are born into a box of space and time, and the movies come closer than any other art form in giving us the experience of walking in someone else's shoes. They allow us an opportunity to experience what it would be like to live within another gender, race, religion, nationality, or period of time. They expand us, they improve us, and sometimes they ennoble us. They also thrill us and make us laugh and cry, and for that gift, and for that, I am very grateful.

INKSPOTS AND BYLINES. From the time I was a kid, all I ever wanted was to be a newspaperman. At sixteen, I started writing full-time at the *Champaign-Urbana News-Gazette*. Right out of college, I was hired at *Chicago Sun-Times* and made their film critic at a very young age. That set me up for the rest of my career—the Pulitzer in 1975, the TV work with Gene Siskel, the star on the Hollywood Walk of Fame in 2005. You never know how long you've got, but newspapers have been good to me for forty-two years (and counting).

BROTHERS FROM ANOTHER MOTHER. My old buddy and reviewing partner, Gene Siskel, and I were often told we had a sibling rivalry, and both thought we were the older brother. I miss him.

THUMBS AND STARS. They're both basically silly, but they *are* useful shorthand. Nothing says "it stinks" like a downturned thumb. Everybody understands that.

WRITE TO LIFE. Writing affirms me and keeps me connected to people and useful, too, and I love the process of writing itself. It's one way that I have survived a very serious illness, four major surgeries, and many complications.

THE KEY TO SURVIVAL. Just do the next right thing, and be grateful for the chance you have to go do that. It's *that* simple. *Really*.

ONE GOOD WOMAN. Movies and writing have, probably literally, kept me alive, but I've been completely looked after by my wife of eighteen years, Chaz. She was my guardian angel during my illness. She is a bottomless well of love and encouragement, for which I am endlessly grateful. We really *do* need someone in our corner.

Jonathan Safran Foer
on gratitude

*"I'm grateful for anything
that reminds me of what's
possible in this life.
Bruno Schulz's book,* Street of
Crocodiles, *does that for me."*

GREATER MINDS HAVE SNAPPED PENCILS, shorn forests, and lost faith approaching the atrocities of the Holocaust and September 11, 2001 in fiction, but then Don DeLillo has never written with a child's heart and Philip Roth has never employed cartoons and flipbooks in his novels. Now in his thirties, Jonathan Safran Foer—the bestselling author of *Everything Is Illuminated,* a poignant *and* madcap exploration of his family's very personal connection to the tragedies of World War II, and *Extremely Loud and Incredibly Close,* a winsome, precocious, and fragile story of one child's grief in the shadow of the fallen towers—has already established himself as a virtuoso, an ambitious and audacious literary stylist, a dazzling storyteller, a dream weaver and spellbinder, and a pyrotechnician of the human spirit. Janet Maslin of the *New York Times* says Safran Foer "combine(s) inspired mischief with a grasp of the unthinkable."

Today, we may perceive the slight, bespectacled author as something of a boy wonder, but it was only two decades ago that he was, like so many prodigious artists, suffering a crippling childhood as the result of a classroom chemical accident at age eight that nearly killed him. In 2005, he told the *Times* that the accident left him wanting nothing except to be outside his own skin. But a Princeton creative writing course, shepherded by Joyce Carol Oates, forever altered the destiny of Safran Foer—her praise, support, and encouragement helped lead the young author to pursue a career in letters faithfully and energetically. A 1999 Ukrainian odyssey provided the grist for Safran Foer's 2002 debut, *Illuminated*, which intoxicated publishers, critics, and readers alike. Almost a decade later, Safran Foer remains one of his generation's most intriguing artists, not only capable of virtually anything, but likely to try it, too. He lives in Brooklyn with his wife, novelist Nicole Krauss, and their two children. His most recently published book, *Eating Animals*, is nonfiction. It reveals his lifelong experiences with vegetarianism—something else not attempted by DeLillo or Roth.

SOME *WUNDERKIND* OF WONDERFUL. The success of my first book, *Everything Is Illuminated*, allowed me at a very early age to have control of my time and my purpose, and all but guaranteed that I would have a second book published—which is something I never remotely took for granted. I was an author all of a sudden. And it felt really good. I hope I would have been just as grateful for the *experience* of writing the book even if it had been utterly trashed or ignored.

FOLLOWING THE MUSE. I often write in risky and experimental ways, but it's because that's really the way I think the story should be told—not because I'm trying to challenge a model or be clever. I'm not trying to ruffle feathers or aggressively change the way things are done; I'm simply honoring the story. I think that's important.

THE Z CHANNEL. Since having children, I've become, occasionally, fairly sleep-deprived, and what I've learned is, the ability to think creatively is the first thing to go. Writing is one of the most fundamental things to my sense of myself, but doing it is like icing on life's cake. When I'm tired or unhealthy or stressed out or hungry, that icing is the first thing to go, and I miss it when it does—because icing is good. So sleep is good, too. I'm grateful for sleep.

A MOVABLE FEAST. Anytime someone has a kind of ritual in their lives—which is a particular, deliberate choice of routine—it's beautiful to me. I may not agree with the particularities of their choices—be they religious, or otherwise—but I'm also a little bit jealous. They have more opportunities to be deliberate as to how they move through the world. For me, I make food choices—and being a vegetarian—a way of being deliberate and mindful about my world. Eating can be so mechanical, something for which one feels exactly nothing. We eat merely to get full. It's nice to have a way to think about it, and eating a certain way brings that ritual and meaning to an aspect of my life.

THE ART OF POSSIBILITY. I'm grateful for anything that reminds me of what's possible in this life. Books can do that. Films can do that. Music can do that. School can do that. It's so easy to allow one day to simply follow into the next, but every once in a while we encounter something that shows us that anything is possible, that dramatic change is possible, that something new can be made, that laughter can be shared. Bruno Schulz's book, *Street of Crocodiles*, does that for me.

LIVE POETS SOCIETY. I like being around so much energy and creativity. The energy of my students at NYU really feeds me. That energy is really one of the most important things for a writer to have. Joyce Carol Oates taught me that. Often, I will leave my class wanting to write, feeling almost new to it. That's a blessing.

MENTAL TWILIGHT. There are not many moments in my day from the time I wake up, especially now that I have children, until about nine at night, when my thoughts become entirely my own. It's very rare that we're not doing something or preparing to do something. It's important to really pay attention to those in-between moments. It's like mental twilight, where you just *are* for a moment. Sometimes I'll count the minutes backwards. It's when I've got a moment to myself that I can best appreciate all the things that surrounded me in my day.

THAT WHICH REMAINS. I'm grateful for everything that isn't falling apart. There's a great passage in *Moby Dick* where Melville talks about how you don't always appreciate the warmth of your bed unless some part of your body is exposed. I feel lucky right now that no part of my body is exposed and that I can be grateful for that.

Morgan Freeman
on gratitude

" . . . I appreciate being older
when I became successful.
It granted me a good deal
of perspective . . . ."

HE HAS PROVIDED A VOICE FOR GOD, and a face
sometimes, too, at least on the silver screen, and with each utter-
ance—sometimes divine, other times malevolent—audiences
hold their breath. When Morgan Freeman speaks, we listen.
He's got *that* kind of a voice: an instrument of grace, wisdom,
and experience. It is the voice, as it turns out, of one who listens; for whom consciousness matters. If God is in the details,
then Freeman has spent a lifetime cascading light—if not deep
analysis—on life's finer emotional and spiritual points. It is with
immediacy and clockwork precision that Freeman is able to
recount stories of movie theater marathons as a seven-year-old
in Chicago, his improbable introduction to the footlights, and,
years later, time on the Broadway stage in an all-black version of
Hello Dolly. Today, five Oscar nominations and one win later (for
2004's *Million Dollar Baby*), it's easy to think that Freeman—like

the deity he portrayed in *Bruce Almighty* and *Evan Almighty*—has always been here. But Freeman does not shy away from revealing the details of his leaner hours, those closer to midnight . . . his scrappy childhood, his difficult years between playing Count Dracula and Easy Reader on PBS's *Electric Company* and establishing credibility in Hollywood with such movies as *Street Smart*, *Driving Miss Daisy*, *The Shawshank Redemption*, *Glory*, and *Invictus*. You get the sense that Freeman knows what it's like to hunt and what it's like to be hunted (watch *Street Smart* or *Unforgiven* to bare witness to his shattering on-screen volatility), yet his approach is always even-handed. The brow does not furrow on Freeman, on-screen or off, which means, perhaps, that he blinks with the eyes of a poet. He certainly speaks with that voice.

THE POWER OF ONE. Providence has much to do with how your life unfurls. Providence provides opportunity. Your job is to exploit it to the best of your abilities. One of the things that occurred to me quite a while back is that I have to be very careful about what I wish for, because it always seems to come true.

THE PICTURES GOT SMALLER. I was just a kid, back in the mid-'40s, living in Chicago, when I started going to the movies every day. Tickets were five cents, and the theaters showed three features. You could be there all day. I used to go to The Virginia and The Indiana all the time. An empty quart milk bottle would sell back then for a nickel. A bottle of Coca-Cola or a small beer bottle would sell for two cents. I was a hoarder of bottles when I was a kid. That's how I paid my way into the movies. That's how I "met" Cagney and Bogart and Coburn.

THE ACTING BUG. In grade school, I pulled a chair out from under a girl named Barbara Curry. Of course, that made her extremely angry, so I had to run, and I was caught by my English teacher, Miss Cosburn. She frog-marched me to the classroom of another English teacher, who was looking for somebody to be in a play that was going to compete in a statewide contest. I did the play, we won the contest, and I became an actor. That's how life works.

UP, UP, AND AWAY. Three years, eight months, and ten days that made up a very formative experience for me. I enlisted in the Air Force for two reasons: One, as a movie buff, I had my romance with violence and gunplay, thanks to the westerns. I was very strongly attracted to the idea of being a fighter pilot. And, two, how do you come out of the small town you grew up in? I was ready to leave Mississippi, and the Air Force was my ticket out. That's how I started seeing the world with my own eyes.

BODIES, REST, AND MOTION. There's that saying about it being darkest right before the dawn. There's a lot of truth in that. I hadn't worked in a couple of years, back in the late '70s, early '80s. I was thinking about going out and getting a real job. Then a friend of mine got sick and had to bow out of his job on (the soap opera) *Another World*. I replaced him. That's just luck. And then there's that other saying: When you got, you get. That job led to another job to another job to another job, and it didn't stop after that.

TABLOID TERRORS. You need only look at today's news to see how wild, unbridled success—coming when you're young and foolish, two things that often come together—can be a great detriment to a talented person. In my case, I appreciate being older when I became successful. It granted me a good deal of perspective by which to enjoy the success, but with humility.

MUTUAL ADMIRATION SOCIETY. The great joy of being in the position I'm now in is I'm always meeting heroes. I'm still a child of the movies, and so I still get a little starstruck when I meet someone like Clint Eastwood or Robert Redford or Jack Nicholson. And then I get to work with them! It's such a great joy, and such a privilege. You're always going, "Wow, here I am." I've never gotten over that.

NELSON MANDELA. Mentor? Yeah. Role model? It's hard to say that about Nelson Mandela. It's like saying "God is a role model." (*laughs*) Years ago, Mandela wrote his autobiography and named me as the actor he would like to play him in the movie. We didn't make that movie, but I *did* get to play him, and that was an enormous blessing.

DO RE ME AL GREEN. Not to the exclusion of anyone else, but Al Green really stands out for me. I sing along with him every chance I get. How could I *not*?

THE BIG BLUE. I have a little yacht, and I take it out every chance I get. Approaching the sea is a genuine encounter. It's one of the places on this earth where you really see who you are, deep inside. The sea is capable of taking you to places of incredible beauty and incredible terror, sometimes very close together. Everyone should experience that. You learn a lot about yourself in those times.

Neil Gaiman
on gratitude

"Both in good fiction and in life, you may not always get what you want, but you will probably get what you need. We should be grateful for these things."

THERE HAVE BEEN MEN IN BLACK BEFORE, Johnny Cash for sure and those blockbuster-prone alien hunters, but none like Neil Gaiman. Pale of complexion, with a raven shock of black hair, his frame draped always in inky midnight, Gaiman is a walking study in chiaroscuro, suggesting he is both a Cash-like outlaw and, quite possibly, a visitor from another planet. At the very least, he's a Brit in Middle America. Gaiman is also one of this generation's seminal creative artists. With Alan Moore (*Watchmen*) and Frank Miller (*The Dark Knight Returns*), Gaiman became part of a triumvirate of rabid, genius writers who reinvented comic books in the 1980s, dispensing with leotards and onomatopoeia in favor of subterranean storytelling, myth-infused narratives, characters that were rich or mad with fever, passion, and disturbance, and a level of sophistication that was not only more mature than your grandfather's Superman, but was actually *literary*. Gaiman's *Sandman* series—the epic tale of Morpheus, Lord of Dreams, who escapes long imprisonment to rebuild his kingdom in the modern world—was praised by none other than Norman Mailer as "a comic book for intellectuals." Sandman, tragic, romantic, satiric, and endlessly inventive, made Gaiman, a self-described "geeky English Jew," into a rock star—a status he embraced by connecting with his fans every which way he could. He is a regular fixture at comic book conventions, has kept an active blog for more than a decade, and "tweets" with an almost supernatural frequency and wit. For his encore, Gaiman moved to America, ditched the drawings altogether, and has become one of our most compelling authors, penning bestselling novels like *Stardust*, *American Gods*, as well as work for children like *Coraline* and *The Graveyard Book*. At fifty, he is also an in-demand filmmaker, rapidly becoming a Renaissance man (in black, natch), working with Robert Zemeckis on 2008's *Beowulf* redo and earning an Oscar nomination for the stop-motion visual treat, *Coraline*. Like the man himself, Gaiman's stories crackle with eccentricity and wisdom, a puckish—possibly dangerous—sense of humor, and an appreciation for the arcane and long forgotten. Soft-spoken, his every phrase considered carefully and delivered polished like a glass figurine or a secret spell, Gaiman is an extraordinary conversationalist—a soothsayer and a magician, a shape-shifter too, wholly aware of the blessings he has received in this life. When we spoke it was merely days after he had proposed marriage to his girlfriend Amanda Palmer, lead singer of the Dresden Dolls, and he seems to be born again, always in black, but in the name of love.

THE COLOR OF MY TRUE LOVE'S HAIR. I love the color black, but probably for completely different reasons than anyone might assume. I love it for how incredibly simple it makes dressing. That's really all there is to it. People tell me that Albert Einstein had nine suits and ties, sets, that were all exactly the same, and, "Oh, isn't that weird?"—*No*. That makes *complete* sense to me, of course. You get up in the morning and you don't think about what you're going to wear. That detail's already been handled. When I was young, I decided to go monochrome—gray, really—thinking that would simplify things. It hadn't occurred to me then that there were blue grays and brown grays and greenish grays and pure grays. I would put on these things and I would look a mismatched mess. Whereas black, it takes care of you.

THE USES OF ENCHANTMENT. Both in good fiction and in life, you may not always get what you want, but you will probably get what you need. We should be grateful for these things.

REAL LOVE, PART I. In my case, love today comes with having a very good idea of who I am and what I want and what would make me happy, which when you're a kid you genuinely don't know. You go, "This person is pretty!" (*laughs*) "Oh, this person seems to like me. That hasn't happened before!" And you're happy to do that thing that people do in cartoons, where their eyes roll up in their heads and they float off the ground six inches and fall forward a little bit. A friend of mine quoted a statistic to me the other day about the divorce rate, which has consistently hovered at about 50 percent for many, many years. But if you exclude marriages from people under the age of thirty, and simply look at people who waited until they were thirty or older to be married, the divorce rate drops to virtually zero. With Amanda, pretty much from the moment I fell in love with her, I also was completely certain that I would happily marry her and happily spend the rest of my life with her. After that, it was only a matter of waiting and seeing if she came to the same conclusion.

SOMEWHERE IN MIDDLE AMERICA. Last night, when I walked the dog, here in Wisconsin, it was minus 15 degrees—minus 26 with the wind chill, according to the weather site. Tonight, I'm going to Los Angeles with survivor's guilt, feeling very badly for all of the people I'm leaving behind in this cold. Having said that, even walking last night at minus 26, the air was so preternaturally clear, the moon was actually doing that "shining bright as day" thing, the shadows fell just perfectly to the snow, and the stars looked like they'd been draped by a Hollywood set designer. The beauty, even as my skin—where it was exposed to the cold air—actually hurt, was still so overwhelming and so peaceful. That's a blessing.

ORTHODOX HUMOR. I remember reading a joke one day, as a child, in *The Joys of Yiddish* by Leo Rosten. An uneducated man is without his prayer book one night, far from home. He knows he needs to say his prayers, but he's left his prayer book far behind. He looks up at God and says, "You know, You, You're so much better than I am at all of this stuff. So I'll tell you what: I'll say the alphabet and you just put the letters together in the right order." One week later, my cantor was telling me this joke as if it had really happened. I'm not sure which is funnier, but I know I wanted to believe him.

ONCE UPON A TIME. One of the best things for me about getting to write for children is trying to fill them with the idea that they live in a world of infinite possibility. For me, as a child, books were an escape. The local library was an escape. Books were places, and I mean that very, very literally. Books were places I went if I felt powerless, if the world was a bit much. . . . As children, one of the key things *is* that sense of powerlessness. Lacking the ability to control one's environment, one seeks out a good, safe place. One goes to a safe, good place that tells you about the world that you live in — big, true things about the world you live in.

THE KINDNESS OF STRANGERS: REAL LOVE, PART II. Amanda is not the kind of girl who does what she is told, and I am, oddly, most grateful to a man whose name I do not know whom we met walking home together last Christmas. This man was playing loud Christmas carols on his saxophone on the bridge, and he stopped Amanda. I assumed it was a fan or someone who simply wanted a chat. They had a moment together, and I asked, "Well, what was that about?" And she said, "He told me that I was incredibly beautiful and young, and that I shouldn't be with an old guy like you." At first, I wanted to go back and pelt him, but she stopped me and said, "No, it's very good for me to be told what not to do, because then I start thinking about what I *do* want to do." Sometimes you only find out what you think when you're called upon to defend it. I'm incredibly grateful to the man on the bridge for telling her what not to do.

SIMPLICITY. The glory of being a writer is as fundamental as having something to write with and something to write on. I adore that simplicity.

CALAMANSI JUICE. It is *absolutely* awesome. It's one of those things. It's not a lime. It's not an orange. It's absolutely its own thing. It's a citrus flavor, but it's unique and quite marvelous. I don't know why it just exists in the Philippines. There's a whole world, this underground world of calamansi juice. They slip it to me at signings. They go, "I'm Philippino; here's some calamansi juice." (*laughs*) It's true.

HAPPILY EVER AFTER: REAL LOVE, PART III. New Year's Eve, last year, it was Amanda Palmer and the Boston Pops—a big show, huge, biggest thing in Boston. Amanda had been so nervous. She hadn't eaten for a couple of days beforehand. During the course of the Boston Pops gig, champagne was poured. Afterward, there was more champagne. She did that thing where you're using champagne as a food substance, without actually noticing that it also contains alcohol—which meant that when she woke up New Year's Day she was incredibly happy, which lasted about an hour and a half, until we got out to breakfast with her father and brother and stepmother. She sort of excused herself to be sick and wasn't actually eating her breakfast and as we walked home, she looked incredibly sad and was incredibly hung over and that was the point where I realized, "I *really* love her. Even with a headache and a hangover, I really love this girl." So I went down on one knee, in the snow, and asked her to marry me, and she said yes. I got up and then I realized, "Wait a minute, we're meant to do rings and things. Damn, we're completely not doing this properly." So I got out this black Sharpie pen from my pocket and I drew a ring on her finger. Because I was facing her, I got the wrong hand. Next morning, I drew a ring on the correct finger; it was bigger—more bling. Day three, I got even more bling. (*laughs*) I've just resigned myself to a future in which I would draw rings on her finger every morning forever.

Ricky Gervais
on gratitude

"Without empathy,
you've got nothing."

TO PARAPHRASE STEVE MARTIN, comedy isn't pretty, and Ricky Gervais knows it well. The forty-nine-year-old Brit, creator of *The Office* and *Extras*, is, in real life, an everyman of the first order—the anti-Hugh Jackman, if you will. Nothing perfect. And yet, as a craftsman, Gervais achieves the sublime over and over again by shining an empathetic, not to mention unflinchingly funny, light on the imperfections of human beings like *The Office's* David Brent and *Extras's* Andy Millman. These are contemporary Scrooges—ego-centered blowhards who harm the ones they love most—but who are always hilariously on the road to a modest redemption (even if it's against their will). Just like you and me. While Gervais's *Office* becomes the unlikeliest of international franchises (with adaptations currently storming the airwaves in France, Germany, Brazil, and Chile), and his riotous talk show claims the Guinness record for the world's most downloaded podcast, Gervais is quietly forging a career as one of the twenty-first century's more interesting artists. Raised in a happy, Waltonsesque family, he claims, Gervais studied philosophy in college, and could very well have gone the way of Wham's Andrew Ridgley, thanks to a one-album recording career in the Britpop duo, Seona Dancing. Years of work on radio and at the BBC resulted in two of the most important relationships in Gervais's life—with creative partner Stephen Merchant and life partner Jane Fallon—which provided a launch pad for his celebrated television series *The Office*. In conversation, Gervais is thoughtful and reflective one moment, rambunctious the next, blunt like a skillet to the back of the head for a minute, then Jerry Lewis goofy for a second. Talking with Gervais is like enjoying the least boring day in the world.

COMEDY PLUS. It's one thing to make people laugh, but it's something else to make that laughter resonate. If you can make people laugh *and* feel something, and do it without schmaltz and formula, then I think you've aimed higher. It's comedy plus. It's what I try to do, and it requires empathy. Without empathy, you've got nothing. I can't laugh at someone I don't like. I can't care about someone I don't like.

BULLETPROOF BLOKE. I have always believed I would walk away from the business. When I first started out as an actor, when I first got into television, when I first got into film, I *will* walk away. It's never been a bluff. You rarely come across people who really mean it. It makes me pretty bulletproof. I feel like a suicide bomber. There's nothing you can hold over me.

SWIMMING IN THE MAINSTREAM. Some of my favorite films are big, accessible Hollywood stories. I love *The Godfather* and *Casablanca* —great stories, acted well, made well. I don't want to make depressing, gritty, urban stories that are depressing to watch. I don't want to make movies that are oppressively artsy or avant-garde. I want to give people something to enjoy. When people think I'm a control freak and an ogre — which I am—it's only because I want my work to be accessible and everyman, in a way.

TROUSERS UP. There's no difference between fame and infamy. Instead of becoming better actors, too many artists simply become better disasters in hopes of becoming bigger celebrities. You drop your trousers in public, and you don't need to be talented to get noticed. Why not work hard and get better at something? I don't know a thing about Robert DeNiro. I don't know where he lives or who he sleeps with or what his favorite color is, and I don't care. He's brilliant. That's all I need to know. These people live their lives like an open wound, and I always think, "Really? You can never take all of that back? Life isn't a blackboard. This is part of your legacy now."

BASIC INSTINCTS. Initially, you do your work intuitively. I never approached my work academically. I just did what I liked and did my best. I've done a lot of things right without really knowing it, if you know what I mean. One thing that's always resonated with me, that I've understood more as I've worked more, is redemption. And I think forgiveness is, possibly, the most wonderful virtue you can give yourself or another. Growing up, I thought integrity was most important, but it is sometimes a luxury. *Everyone* can forgive.

I CAN'T. I'M BUSY. The only time I lie now is for the peace of mind of myself and others. I lie two or three times a week, and this is the only lie I've told for, probably, the last twenty years: "Can you come to my party Saturday?" "No, I can't. I'm busy." That is the lie I tell often, and almost exclusively. It's so much easier—and nicer—than saying, "Don't know you enough, don't like you enough, would rather sit at home in my pants watching television than be anywhere near your party." That's when the truth is worse than a lie, and I'm glad I told you so.

DRESSED FOR SUCCESS. I've started wearing pajamas out, because they're more comfortable than trousers. I'm so grateful for pajamas. (*laughs*) I started out with jeans, then went to sweat pants about ten years ago. Now it's just pajamas. I wore them to the White House. I've gone whole hog.

Nikki Giovanni
on gratitude

"Go out and fall in love. The worst it's going to be, falling in love, is you get poems."

IF YOU DO NOT WISH TO EVOLVE, do not read the work of poet Nikki Giovanni. It will change you. It changed *her*. Coming of age at the front lines of the '60's racial and social cacophony, every day a protest, a setback, a riot, or assassination, Giovanni—well-loved as a child, and even better educated—turned bad into verse, becoming a spokesperson of sorts for her generation, a rebel with a cause. Her voice was fearsome, her style informal and electrifying, her reach far and wide. Her early books of poetry, 1967's *Black Feeling, Black Talk*; 1968's *Black Judgment*; and 1970's *Re: Creation*, backed by nearly evangelical public readings in New York's jazz and blues clubs, were militant, galvanizing, revolutionary, and full of rage—which was only Giovanni's hope for utopia pressed to bleeding into rhyme. They were also enormously successful, selling tens of thousands of copies—unheard of, then and now, for books of poetry. In

1969, Giovanni gave birth to Thomas Watson Giovanni, her only child, whom she has raised as a single mother. Parenthood, she said, altered her perception of the world and her place in it. The radical voice of protest against social injustice evolved into a warmer search for beauty and connectedness, albeit one frequently infused with frustration, loss, and loneliness. Intensity is a Giovanni trademark, whether she is championing the rap maestro Tupac Shakur (as she often did and does), addressing a departed lover, or convincing her lung cancer—diagnosed in 1995—to sign a truce that allows them to live peacefully together for another thirty years. More recent volumes of poetry, like *Acolytes* and *Bicycles: Love Poems*, are intimate, soul stirring, richly specific, and awesomely universal at once. In conversation from her office at Virginia Tech, where she has been a Distinguished Professor of English since 1987, Giovanni is frequently funny—possessed of a firecracker wit, an elegance of tongue that can suddenly, surprisingly turn salty, and a reverent demeanor that can still spring to rebellious life. Turns out, Giovanni is still a rebel with a cause, but that cause has turned, finally, to love itself, a turn she anticipated in the poem, "When I Die," which reads in part:

and if ever I touched a life I hope

that life knows that I know that touching was and still is and will always

be the true

revolution.

When you begin to quote the passage aloud to her, she joins you, her voice merging with yours, and the poem is all of a sudden a duet, impromptu, unexpected, *connected*, which is how Giovanni, you think, always meant her work to be.

LIVING OUT LOUD. I'm a part of the civil rights generation, and we thought about making political change. That kind of change is sometimes possible, but not because of a poem or a play or a song; it's possible because people put their bodies on the line. And we've seen, historically, the results of that. As an artist, you can't make people face a water hose;

you can only record it. I've always considered my job to be the voice of a people without a voice, and to make it as personal as I can.

FEARLESSNESS. Remember that movie *The Gods Must Be Crazy?* It's funny. I'm that person—the Coke bottle would've fallen on my head. But you can't be safe in this life. You can't run your whole life thinking you could be safe. Nobody's safe, and that's not what's given to you. What you're given is this life, for as long as you have it. Whenever you lose it, you will not like that. You can live to 120, and you'll still be saying, "Oh, I wish I had a few more years." You might get on a brand new airplane on a beautiful day, on your way to adventures, and the pilot for reasons totally unknown makes the wrong turn and you're dead. You have to live your life completely. You can't be thinking, some Arab's gonna come out here and get me or some Islamic's gonna get me. No one's out to get you. The nature of life is: Someday you're gonna lose it. So you'd better live it. And you can't live afraid. Do not be ruled by fear.

HIP-HOP NATION. I'm very fond of the hip-hop nation. They're trying to tell the truth. I still miss Tupac Shakur. I think we all do, or we should. He was always telling the truth, and he was totally, totally courageous. There was just no bend in that young man. But we also have Kanye West, whom I believe to be a stand-up man, very courageous. I love Ice-T and Queen Latifah, too. The hip-hop nation can get a little tired when all they talk about is sex—there are only so many ways you can do it and only so many ways you can cum, and then it's over. I'm not knocking it, it's just, "Guys, guys, guys, go to community college and read a book. There's something else out there besides your penis, as it were." But these are the poets of today. I think poetry is in as good of shape as opera today. Nobody questions opera. Less than 10 percent of the country listens to it; it's a subject on *Jeopardy*, so is poetry. I think hip-hop should be. It's all telling the truth.

BEWITCHED, BOTHERED, AND BEWILDERED. I'm a poet. I'm always in love. I write better when I'm in love. I made a discovery that's not a secret; being in love's not necessarily about somebody being in love with you. If you were always waiting for somebody to love you back, you might never be in love. So what you do is you fall in love with somebody and you write these lovely love poems, and it doesn't matter if the person even knows you exist. Go out and fall in love. The worst it's going to be, falling in love, is you get poems. You might not be able to see straight when you're falling in love. You might say, "Oh, shit, this is a mistake." You're a writer, so you're going to suffer. But at least you get those poems, and at least one of them is going to be good. So there's no downside to love. And it makes your skin look better, too.

THE BEAUTY OF PASSING YEARS. I've enjoyed my twenties and my thirties and forties, but if I were picking *my* time, I'm totally in love with my sixties. I don't know what people are bitching and moaning about. I know I'll wake up one day and have Alzheimer's or something, but right now I'm writing with a deeper intensity than I ever have. My book *Acolytes*, it was written at my mother's bedside, on my laptop, as she was in her last days. These are not poems about "Mommy," per se, but about loss and what you do with irreparable loss. And I couldn't have written that book when I was any age but what I am right now.

Dave Grohl

on gratitude

"Anytime something good happens,
it's always, like,
'God, how could my life get any
better than it already is?'"

SOMETIMES TRAGEDY IS A STRAITJACKET, and other times it's a cape. If you're Dave Grohl, born in 1969, shaggy front-man of the multiplatinum Foo Fighters and the recently formed super group Them Crooked Vultures, not to mention the skin pounder behind Nirvana's grunge masterpieces *Nevermind* and *In Utero*, you simply accept that bad things sometimes happen to good people, count your blessings or your lucky stars, then find another impossible dream to fulfill. This is the kid, after all, who discreetly learned how to play drums by slamming pillows with chopsticks, honed his guitar playing skills on campus (Circle Jerks tunes preferred), and joined his first band—Freak Baby, for the record—when he was only sixteen. That Grohl, widely considered one of the nicest guys in rock music, would end up in the Nirvana rocket ship—nay, powder keg—is only to say he was in the right place at the right time, and he's grateful for it.

Grohl's inspired timekeeping lent a splashy, tribal-punk urgency to Kurt Cobain's crunchy chaos. And without further ado, enter grunge—a genre was born. Only three years into the journey, Cobain penned a fatal exeunt in heroin and gunpowder. Undeterred, but humbled, Grohl became a one-man band, recording fourteen of his own original songs under the UFO-inspired moniker Foo Fighters. Before releasing the Foo's 1995 debut, Grohl drafted a full band, its lineup largely intact a decade and a half and some 15 million albums later. Alternating stardom with domestic bliss, Grohl is a happily married father to two young daughters, Violet Maye and Harper Willow, but still and always a superhero.

FOR THOSE ABOUT TO ROCK (WE SALUTE YOU). I saw AC/DC's concert movie, *Let There Be Rock*, circa 1979, and that changed everything for me. It really made me want to become a rock musician—not necessarily as a career, but to get back at all the people I hated in high school. (*laughs*) Rock 'n' roll is the greatest revenge. There's no question.

HAPPY ACCIDENTS. I never imagined music being a career. I was just a suburban kid who worked at a furniture warehouse all week long so I could play music on the weekends, never in bands that had any real commercial potential. It was playing from the heart, and noisy. (*laughs*) It was never about being a rock star or making money. And then Nirvana happened, and I just laughed for a year. I thought, "Oh my God, this is ridiculous!" The Foo Fighters was the same thing. It started with me doing a demo in five days in my house, which then kind of turned into a band that's been around for fifteen years. We've never had a world domination attitude or plan. I've never for one second felt like I deserve any of this. Anytime something good happens, it's always, like, "God, how could my life get any better than it already is?"

MAKING NANCY REAGAN PROUD. I just said no to an awful lot of stuff, but I did my share of partying until I was, like, twenty. (*laughs*) It was fun for a while, but I got over it. It didn't feel good for me. As a musician, you're surrounded by that, and that lifestyle, and you've gotta watch your step. I've seen it happen over and over and over again. It's the most cliché pitfall, and it can happen to anybody. As soon as a musician gets close to needles, it's all over, man. If you're into making music and going out and sharing with people, that's your number one priority.

VIOLET VAUDEVILLE. She looks like my wife and acts like me, which is a nuclear combination. I'm in trouble, for sure. (*laughs*) She's going to be a six-foot-tall supermodel with a really wicked sense of humor and a Mensa IQ. It's going to be tough. (*laughs*) Violet can work a room like Billy Crystal, I swear. It's the Violet Maye Grohl show every night, and no two shows are ever the same. She's out of her mind.

FOUR SEASONS IN ONE DAY. I look at pictures of myself when I was eighteen years old. You know what I was wearing? Vans, jeans, and T-shirts. I'm forty-one now, and I look exactly the same—except I'm carrying some bags under my eyes. And I can grow a beard. (*laughs*) As you get older, you start to realize that you don't know shit. When you're a kid, you think you know it all. Now, I realize how little I do know. One thing I've learned, it's that I have to stretch my days. Life is too short to sleep in. Life is too short to wish tomorrow came sooner. I wish that every day was twenty-eight hours long. I can't seem to fit all the things I want to do into one day.

WITH A LITTLE HELP FROM MY FRIENDS. When Nirvana became huge, I spent a lot of time hanging out back in Virginia with my childhood friends, instead of partying with strippers and miles of cocaine. I stayed with my buddies. The Foo Fighters road crew today, it's the same thing; they're like family. When I walk up on stage, every single guy that works for us, they're working hard to give us a good show. And we're doing the same thing for them. We take care of each other. It's a beautiful thing. When you spend a year and a half on the road, it helps to be out there with your friends. It's hard to be out there in Bologna, Italy, with a day off and no company but yourself. You feel lost in space. But when you're there with twenty of your best friends, it makes all the difference. I'd do anything for those guys, and they'd do anything for us.

KNOW WHEN TO HOLD 'EM, AND WHEN TO FOLD 'EM. I'm an optimist, so I can see the good in almost anything. There are some things that are so tragic that they're hard to reconcile, or it's hard to see the good in them. But I believe you can learn from even the worst things in life. Kurt (Cobain's suicide) is a hard thing to talk about. If I had my choice, Kurt would still be alive. If I could change one thing, it would be that. But you play the hand you're dealt. That's it. I can't spend my life wishing things were different. I'm just playing what I've got with everything I've got.

"HOME." My wife bought me a piano for my birthday (a couple years ago). I had never played piano before. Someone sat me down and said, "That there, that's middle C." From there, I started figuring out how to make chords, and "Home" is the first song I wrote on a piano. I used to be able to travel light, pick up, and leave for months and months on end. Now, I have a beautiful wife, beautiful daughters, a beautiful life, and I've realized that home isn't necessarily a place. It's not the house; it's anywhere I am with my wife and daughters. I have this band that sweeps me out every once in a while, and I just try to make my way back home every time. That's what that song is all about. It's a hard song for me to listen to, because it's the first song I've ever written that's absolutely direct, a straight interpretation of how my heart works. Sometimes I wish I could just do a residency in Vegas for the next twenty years of my life, just so I could be close to my wife and daughters all the time. That's what "Home" is all about for me.

Daryl Hall

on gratitude

"I never felt like I had all the tools I needed to be the best. But I always felt like I had enough."

FOR A LOT OF YEARS, Daryl Hall was the Rodney Danger-field of pop music, getting no respect. But whereas the late, great Dangerfield became a sweaty pop culture icon spattering his perennial indignities into riotous, necktie-twisting punch lines, Hall has worked a different kind of mojo as frontman for Hall & Oates, the most commercially successful duo in pop history with more than 60 million records sold and thirty-four *Billboard Magazine* top 100 hits. Perhaps Hall's Nordic good looks, piercing blue eyes, and long blond mane, along with the cheesy hyper-art-directed band aesthetic didn't help the dynamic duo's quest to be taken seriously during their ubiquitous, mid-'80s run on MTV. In fact, it might be only now that you're realizing Daryl Hall penned the soundtrack to your life, or a critical part of it. Tunes like "Sara Smile," "Private Eyes," "Maneater," "Rich Girl," and "I Can't Go For That" are resplendent gems of blue-eyed pop and soul, hooky, buoyant cornucopias of melody, uplift, and universal sentiment. Hall's originals are so good, in fact, you might not realize they're good *for* you too, and yet today, an entire generation of rappers and rockers—from The Killers to Kanye West, Wu Tang Clan to Bird and the Bee—name Hall & Oates a key influence on their work. It was bound to happen sooner or later. Born in 1946 into a Philadelphia-based family of musicians, Hall was by his own admission a "precocious kid," captivated by the chivalric romances of fictional characters like Ivanhoe and Sir Galahad. He was also in love with melody and "howling," crooning for kool kats and frat boys on Saturday nights, then begging for forgiveness with the church ladies on Sunday mornings. By the time he was in high school, Hall was picking up twenty-spots laying down background vocals and keyboard tracks with soul greats like Smokey Robinson, the Temptations, Huff and Gamble, and Chubby Checker. It was at Temple University in the late-'60s that the fates truly intervened, thrusting Hall and John Oates together for the first time in the middle of an on-campus, dancehall knife fight. A kitschy origin story, a genuine *West Side Story* moment, perhaps, and, suddenly, musical kismet occurs. In 2009, Sony Legacy released *Do What You Want, Be What You Are: The Music of Daryl Hall & John Oates*, a four-CD set that collects seventy-four of the duo's best tunes. The boxed-set is a testament to the enduring pop alchemy created by Hall and his most frequent musical collaborator, perennially mustachioed John Oates. For Hall, programming *Do What You Want* was a profound journey of self-discovery. "In the most basic way, putting this boxed set together was like watching home movies. You put on a home movie, you see yourself at eight years old, you go, 'Oh, look at that goofy kid.' You see yourself as people saw you, and that's part of what's cool, but you also hear your own intentions, and *that's* interesting," Hall says, between taping episodes of his web series "Live from Daryl's House" and restoring a 345-year old home in mid-state New York. "In a lot of ways, forty years later, Hall & Oates is enjoying not only a resurgence, but an actual and true discovery of what we're all about, maybe for the first time, and that's something to be really, really grateful for."

BORN LIKE THIS. I learned really early on, like at five or six, how to deal with what everybody calls the fourth wall—with what *performance* is. There's a difference between a performer and a receiver, someone who does and someone who receives. Now it takes two, of course. But learning all of that stuff when I was a kid, coming from the amazing musical family that I did, singing every Sunday in church, it prepared me for what I've done with my life. I never felt like I had all the tools I needed to be the best. But I always felt like I had *enough*. These are good things to know.

SINGING FOR HIS SUPPER. Philadelphia is such an unbelievable melting pot, an amazing place to learn how to create, and it was populated—back when I was a kid—with some of the real greats, guys like Kenny Gamble and Leon Huff and Donny Bell. They took me in, saw me for who I was, and really got me started. They introduced me to a whole world, a scene. They let me in. They put fire in my belly—strength and confidence. They'd put me on recording sessions. I'd hang around the recording studios, telling everybody what I could do, then doing it the best way I could. I was on the B team. They had plenty of A guys, but they'd lay down twenty bucks and drag me in and let me play some keys on their records or let me sing background vocals, until I had the chops to do it on my own. Until I was my own A guy.

CATCH A FALLING STAR. I was lucky, as a teenager, to meet a lot of great people who were just coming off the top of their game—guys, for example, like Chubby Checker, who was the biggest star in the world a few years before I met him (and whose star was very quickly falling when our paths did cross). So I saw things as they were, not in some romantic way. I saw that, no matter how big you were, you were going to go through these inevitable periods of crashing and burning, and I saw how to deal with them. I realized, also, that sheer talent and sheer perseverance, relentlessness and sideways thinking is what keeps people alive in the creative world. Otherwise, you'll crash and burn once, and that's it. I learned these things at a really early age, which allowed me to take all of the things that happened to John (Oates) and me—the ups and downs, and all of that—in stride. I'm grateful for learning all of that as a kid.

MONKEY SEE, MONKEY IMPROVE. Like every artist, I went through periods where I copied from the masters and stole what I needed to. I borrowed from Smokey Robinson when I needed to, and others, too, when I was fourteen or fifteen. But I feel like I got my own style pretty early on, and I can hear myself being me by the time I was sixteen or seventeen. I hear the evolution of what it is to be me—mentally and emotionally—even with this voice I sing with. I had this young kid's voice, and it matured over the years, and it got the way I always wanted it too, really—I got a little more depth. I'm grateful for that.

MAKING ALLEN GINSBERG PROUD. Artists, especially singers, they're very primitive people at their core. I communicate through crying, howling, laughing, and groaning. That's really what music is. It's certainly at odds with people who use their thumbs on keyboards to relay banalities all day long. I don't text; I *howl*.

PENNY LANE. Like any musician, I was out and about for years, but I made a couple of friends that have lasted. There was one friend—a particularly close one in San Francisco. When I'd go there, she'd show me around and really got me into the city of San Francisco. It's things like that that make a lonely person—or a "ghost," as I used to call myself, just kind of floating through peoples' lives for one day, while they're stuck there all the time—feel better, feel connected. I think I've always been grateful to anyone who has made me feel at home. That's a blessing.

THE METHOD OF MODERN LOVE OR, UH, COLLABORATION. When I was a kid, I used to play that drawing game, squiggles. You know, you scribble something on paper—some incomplete line, or something—and you hand it to the next guy and he's gotta finish it. They'd do something with it, and then they'd hand it back to me and I'd build on that. Maybe out of that comes a sort of cartoon or picture. I really loved that game as a kid, and that's the way I like to collaborate.

I like to throw ideas around and go back and forth. It's give and take. I require people with quick ideas, and I've been fortunate to work with some really great people like that in the world of music.

WHEN LYME CAME TO TOWN. I was diagnosed with Lyme disease in 2005. It affects people in all sorts of different ways—chronic arthritis, cognitive problems, brain problems. I got through it all relatively unscathed. I had a hard time for a little bit, but I'm completely functional now. But when you get that kind of diagnosis, you wonder: *Is my career over? Can I work again?* It caused me a lot of anxiety. You never know when Lyme disease is going to flare up or come on you; it's kind of like malaria. You just never know. I could be getting ready for a tour and suddenly have this attack. *Will it mess with my performance or am I only worried that it will*, and then that anxiety sometimes brings the problems on. I've always been a balanced person, but getting sick made me more health-conscious. Getting sick *forced* me to be balanced. I can't abuse myself in any way. In that way, you appreciate good health in a way that I never did before.

THE HOUSE THAT DARYL BUILT. I grew up on construction sites and wandering old, ruined houses with my grandfather and my father, who were handymen. That's good stuff for a kid. As soon as I got the chance, I decided to start renovating old homes. Board by board, stone by stone. It's creation. I'm working on a house now that was built in 1662. That's an old house, man. I build houses now because I spent four decades neither here nor there, always on the road, never having a home, really. My entire adult life, I've been a traveler, a displaced person, itinerant. I never really valued my home space because I was never there. Now I want to save it, preserve it, rebuild it. Home is important these days.

Marcia Gay Harden

on gratitude

*"I'm grateful for the childhood
I had; it prepared me
for the work I do today."*

WHILE RAVEN-HAIRED, AND VOLUPTUOUS, and more often than not, inclined toward darkness, at least in the film roles she chooses, "dark beauty" is, perhaps, too simple a description of Marcia Gay Harden. In conversation, Harden is anything but; she positively glows, emanating an electric intellect, a palpable passion, and an easy, contagious laugh, a lightness that would surprise anyone who knows her only from her harrowing turns in *Pollock, Mystic River,* or *Into the Wild.* If Harden were to write her autobiography, it might well be titled, *The Unbearable Lightness of Being Marcia Gay Harden,* and you'd never be able to put it down. Raised around the world, in a close-knit family by a Naval officer and his wife, Harden always had a flair for theatrics, using all the world as her stage, inventing plays and backyard productions with her sisters, before graduating with an M.F.A. from NYU's renowned Tisch School of the Arts.

Three decades of steady work have found Harden collaborating in virtually every medium with great talents ranging from playwright Tony Kushner to comedian Robin Williams, Clint Eastwood to Drew Barrymore. In 2001, she won an Academy Award for playing the long-suffering Lee Krasner, wife of tortured artist Jackson Pollock. Despite her propensity for plumbing the darker nuances of the human condition in her performances, the real-life Harden celebrates a blissful family life, a happy marriage, an illustrious career, and the thrill of playing hard-to-get with inquiring minds.

THE MILITARY BRAT. I think my childhood, coming from a military family, certainly gave me some training for being an actress. The similarities *are* striking. They're both gypsy lifestyles. You forge really fast, intimate relationships. You learn to surrender to things immediately, and then move on and adapt to the next place, the next situation, the next people. Making movies is so much like that; you're with a group of people who are working on your face, your body, your lighting, your emotions, working together intensely and intimately for three months, and then everybody's gone on to the next thing. I'm grateful for the childhood I had; it prepared me for the work I do today.

SISTER ACT. We used to do plays when I was a kid. We did a lot of front porch theatrics when we were living in Japan, actually. My older sister, Leslie, would hang sheets and clothes along the front porch for a curtain, and we'd sell popcorn to the neighbors and put on these little shows. We were, somehow, a theatrical family, a very playful family, and I have to really give that to my older sister. She got us all involved in doing these plays and finding the fun of it. So this is all *her* fault.

THE BEST GEM UPON HER ZONE. My father was stationed in Greece, so I did my first year of college there. My parents were very much "go see, go do" people, so they were always pushing us out the door. My sisters and I would go explore Athens and we went to the theater at the Parthenon to see plays. I saw *Medea*—so much human emotion, big heights, and great depths. It wasn't kitchen drama; it was so huge, emotionally, lyrically, and it was all under the stars, and people were welling up with tears one moment and then rolling in the aisles with laughter the next. I just fell in love with the theater. How could you not?

THE TROPHY CASE. It's an incredible honor to win an Oscar, so much joy, and a moment I'll never forget. But the next morning? Scripts were not piled up outside my door. People were not pounding down my door wanting to hire me. The lawn was not made of emeralds, which I was sure it would be. Nothing changed, so I just kept doing what I do, making choices that interest me. I went off and did some TV and then a couple of movies that maybe didn't do so well. If you talked to people in the couple of years right after I won the Oscar, they probably would have said I *was* the clichéd Oscar disaster. (*laughs*) But I'm grateful for the trophy.

FREEDOM OF CHOICE. To be honest with you, to be a billionaire and have a mansion with seven pools doesn't hold much interest for me. It sounds like that lifestyle would be completely controlling. I'm not worried so much about being a huge movie star and making billions of dollars. (*laughs*) I want to make choices and take chances that keep me learning, and I'm grateful I've been able to.

FRUITS OF HER LABOR. My family (husband, Thaddeus Scheel, and their three children) lives on a lake in upstate New York. My husband and I, we spend the summer with the kids picking berries, making jam and zucchini bread, and working in the garden. I *love* that, and I'd choose that, even if it meant I can't do other things. I like spending that time with my kids and having them know that tomatoes don't grow on grocery store shelves. (*laughs*) I think that's important.

AN ENIGMA WRAPPED INSIDE A RIDDLE. The more people know about you, the less they can melt into your character, so I think it's important to retain an element of mystery, to keep certain things private. Otherwise, audiences use that knowledge they have of you, in a way. But I don't know that any journalist or interview ever *really* captures a celebrity. What actor is really going to be completely candid with a journalist? (*laughs*) At best, it's all only a *part* of the person. The best interviews, in my opinion, are the ones that are *full* of lies, don't you think? (*laughs*)

Matt Hughes
on gratitude

*"I'm grateful
I was born a champion."*

WHEN YOU'RE A FIGHTER, there's always something to defend. If your last fight was a loss, it's your honor. If you posted a win last match, it's the title you earned. Either way, you're looking to protect the cartilage in your nose and, probably, your two front teeth as well. See, the life of a pugilist means something's always at stake. It could very well be your own life. So when you meet Matt Hughes, the most decorated fighter in the history of the Ultimate Fighting Championship, the billion-dollar empire built around the international appeal of mixed martial arts (MMA) competition, it's somewhat surprising to see how totally *calm* he is. A self-proclaimed country mouse and farm boy from rural Illinois, a hell-raising teenager who channeled his punchy tendencies into a dynamic and lucrative career, Hughes may be placid because of the gilded record he's claimed: fifty wins, seven losses in a decade-long career. But there's something else. It's almost as if Hughes simply knows inchoately that he's the best, keeps it a closely held secret most hours of most days, then leaps into the fabled Octagon to remind everyone what lethal weapons his fists and feet are. Though UFC—which plops bare-knuckled, unscripted MMA bouts into the campy world of Varilites, smoke machines, and casino ka-ching, much like dropping a street fight into Gene Simmons's living room—is a perfect mix of kitsch, histrionics, and actual ass-kicking, Hughes, in all of his serenity, is something of an anomaly. Many UFC fighters tend to the hyperbole of Hulk Hogan—it's good showmanship, after all, catch-phrasing and Neanderthal chest thumping—but the most flamboyant thing about Hughes may be how ordinary he actually is, living on a farm, loving his wife and kids, going to church every Sunday. It's a constant balance, he says, between faith, honor, humility, and gratitude that keeps him on top. Hughes isn't a killer; he only plays one on TV.

CAIN AND ABEL. No matter what, my twin brother Mark's going to be there for me. I've always got someone to watch my back. When we were growing up, we lived miles away from anybody else because we were on this farm out in the middle of nowhere, and so we were always together. I was never lonely. When we got older, that play turned into competition, and that was really engrained into me, that sense of competition. I think I became a really good fighter because my brother was there, and we always pushed each other along. If I got five takedowns, he'd get six. If he'd get six, I'd want seven. It was never ending, the competition between Mark and me. I know that's kept me alive in fights. I'm surely grateful for that.

LOVE THY BROTHER. My brother and I, we fought on the farm, we fought in junior high, we fought in high school, we threw hammers and tools at each other. It was just crazy. One of the great things my dad ever told me, even though I always thought he didn't know anything when I was a teenager, was, and he'd say this as he was pulling my brother and me apart in a fight, "You might not know it, but this is your best friend right here." He knew what he was talking about when he said that.

KING OF PAIN. Every move has a counter, and every counter has a counter. I really have to read my opponent the whole time, figuring out what he's doing and then react to that. That takes thinking. This sport has evolved so much that you can't just go in there and be a Royce Gracie type, where you're doing one thing all the time. You have to do it all. The guy that doesn't know everything is going to be in trouble. I'm grateful I've been a quick learner.

ROUND ONE. My first fight, I knew one thing: I was a wrestler. I didn't figure anybody would beat me wrestling, and if they got close enough to throw a punch at me, then I was close enough to take them down. That was my mentality. As soon as I got people down, they were mine. There wasn't anything anyone could do, once I got them down. I've always known my strengths, and I'm thankful for that. Your strengths *are* your strategy.

BEST OF BOTH WORLDS. Pro wrestling, like WWE, is on one end of the spectrum, and it's 100 percent entertainment. It's not even a sport. It's just entertainment. The outcomes are known ahead of time. It's a show. On the other end of the spectrum, you have boxing, which really has *no* entertainment value; it's just two guys out there, punching each other. That's it. That's 100 percent sport. Then you have UFC, right in the middle. We're 100 percent sport—nothing choreographed, nothing scripted. UFC has never told me what to say or what to do. They've never put anything in my mind at all. I have free reign. At the same time, UFC has great entertainment value—its punches, kicks, strikes, knees, elbows. You never know what's going to happen next, a takedown or submission. We lie right in the middle of boxing and WWE. We've taken down both of those empires by being the best of both worlds, and I'm so grateful to be a part of it.

ALWAYS ONLY ME. Some people come up to me and go, "You're that guy! You're Matt Hughes!" But, really, I'm *just* Matt Hughes. I'm a guy who grew up on the west side of Hillsboro, I love my family and take good care of them, but there's nothing amazing about the guy who gets into the octagon and takes down Frank Trigg. I'm just a guy. But also, if kids are looking for a role model, then here's my story: I'm always trying to do the right thing. It's not that I want kids to look at me and figure out how to act, but some of them are anyway, so I'm living my life by doing the right thing. I'm not trying to be somebody; I just *am* somebody.

SPIRITUAL WARRIOR. People ask, "How can you be a Christian and be a fighter at the same time?" My response is, "I'm not going in there to beat somebody up. I'm going in there to win." I can win by not throwing a single punch or kick or strike. I can win a lot of ways. The byproduct is, somebody *might* get hurt, but that's not why I'm going out there.

BORN LIKE THIS. Champions are born with a certain mentality. You can take some Joe off the street and no matter how much I work with him, no matter how much experience he's got in the octagon, it doesn't necessarily mean he's going to be good. It doesn't mean he's going to be a champion. But there are other guys who are just competitors, and they don't need a whole lot of training or experience before they're truly great. Right off the bat, they're making good choices without thinking about them. Their natural reactions are exactly right. To be great, you have to know what to do without thinking too much about it. I'm grateful I was born a champion.

Samuel L. Jackson
on gratitude

*"I used the doors
that were shown me, and a lot of
them saved my life."*

SAMUEL L. JACKSON was born again with a Velcro wallet. You know the one: 1994, *Pulp Fiction,* brown wallet on the scummy countertop of a greasy spoon, the inscription: "Bad Motherf****er." If ever a filmmaker offered his star a fitting epitaph, it was there and then, courtesy of *Fiction*'s maestro, Quentin Tarantino. Sure, Jackson had been making movies for almost two decades before *Fiction* launched him to international stardom and an Oscar nomination, but it was the role of righteous hit man Jules Winfield that cemented Jackson in the collective consciousness as a feral, philosophical, big-screen *force majeure*. Once a civil rights activist, an usher at Martin Luther King Jr.'s Atlanta funeral, a Black Power foot soldier, and a long-suffering addict (sober since 1991, two weeks before filming his unforgettable turn as a crackhead in Spike Lee's *Jungle Fever*), Jackson has been to "some pretty dark places." And in spite of it, he has ruled the silver screen with a combination of popcorn (*Snakes on a Plane, Shaft*), legacy (*Star Wars: Episodes I—III*), and prestige (Pixar's *The Incredibles*), which have made him the highest-grossing actor of all time, with nearly $8 billion in ticket sales. Jackson, one of cinema's living icons, able to conjure an omnipotent brew of mystery and menace, has a journeyman's work ethic, a movie star's charisma, and an artist's vast reservoir of soul. Not bad for a self-professed comic-book and anime geek who once worked as Bill Cosby's stand-in. When you meet Jackson in person, you break the ice by challenging him immediately to a staring contest: Jackson once spent months mastering the art of not blinking as a tool for greater screen presence (which he used quite effectively in M. Night Shyamalan's *Unbreakable*). Perhaps because Jackson was raised an only child, he's up for a two-player game and gives it a go, removing his funky, white-framed eyeglasses, laying them deliberately on the table between the two of you, a battle line drawn. And he calls it: "Go." It's a quiet voice, not quite commanding, but in command. If he doubts the outcome in any way, he does not betray it here. He's so focused he's barely breathing. On the other hand, some ninety-two-seconds in, you still haven't blinked either. And then it occurs to you, the tape recorder counter silently marking the time: You've entered into a no-win situation. Either you're the guy who lost a staring contest to Samuel L. Jackson, or you're the guy who beat Samuel L. Jackson in a staring contest. There's really only one way out of this mess. Because even as Jackson is quick to laugh, and a true gentleman, he still embodies some piece of the moniker on the Velcro wallet. So on the count of three . . .

IT'S ALL IN THE EYES. When you don't blink, you possess greater intensity. You can intimidate people. You can let people know you're really into them, that passion thing. You can convey a terror so great that you cannot look away. You communicate everything with your eyes. I can do that.

CHILD'S PLAY. For me, acting is a huge extension of being a kid. I spent my childhood playing war and cowboys and Indians and cops and robbers, jumping out of trees, rolling down hills, playing hide-and-seek, smash and burn. I was just getting ready for my job.

VIOLENCE IS GOLDEN. In my job, I get to do all that James Cagney stuff—shoot, stab, scream, stagger, and fall. It's a boy's life, and it's good for boys to play like that. Plus it lets me work out my kinks. Saves a lot of money lying on someone's sofa.

THE NEW LEAF. I used to wonder if I'd be funny or talented or cool anymore if I was sober. "I won't be the life of the party anymore if I'm sober. No one will like me anymore if I'm sober." But it's this simple: I stopped doing the things I shouldn't, and I started getting all the things I wanted. There's just no contest for me on where I'd rather be.

THE UNUSUAL SUSPECT. There's no honest reason why I shouldn't be in that bad place, hooked on dope, and dying slowly, except something was watching me. I've been in a room full of guys with their guns out, a real bad scene, and one of the guys looks at me says, "Dude, (you were in) *Do the Right Thing*! What the hell are you doing here? Get outta here, man!" Cops have recognized me and sent me out the door during raids. I used the doors that were shown to me back then, and a lot of them saved my life.

CONTROL AND THE ONLY CHILD. Most sports pissed me off growing up because you need more guys, and I was an only child. Even Ping-Pong takes a guy to hit it back to you. Golf is the only game where it's you, this little ball lying still, and the green and the elements: Everything good that happens, it's you; everything bad that happens, it's you. That, I can take. I'm grateful I found golf.

ROLLING WITH IT. Even the best guys miss in golf, almost every time, so the idea is to manage your mistakes and minimize your mistakes. You draw on your skill set and you get there. Some days it's pouring rain. Some days the other guy doesn't know his lines. Some days your swing is lousy. Some days the crew's moving in slow motion. You always have to make your adjustments. That's golf. That's acting. That's life.

BIG B.O. I passed Harrison Ford as the highest grossing actor of all time! I am number one. I'm still beating him down.

Anna Kendrick
on gratitude

"There's a sensitivity that comes with feeling like an outsider at some point in your life."

SHE IS NOT AN EXPERT ON BLUSH or any kind of makeup whatsoever, so please do not ask Anna Kendrick about cosmetics. She would be most grateful if you'd honor that one request, as a thousand journalists failed to during her recent madcap, coiffed-and-rouged rush of the awards circuit, having been nominated for an Oscar for her star-making work in *Up in the Air*. And still, if you did ask, Anna Kendrick would probably answer intelligently, and with a smile. Not because it's good for business, but because she believes it's important to be kind. Even to idiot reporters. At twenty-five, Kendrick is an overnight success in twelve short years, having made her Broadway debut as a preteen, doing a round of Sondheim, appearing in a run of independent films, portraying the gossipy Jessica Stanley in the *Twilight* franchise, and then her spectacular work as Natalie Kenner in *Air*. Born and raised in Portland, Maine, always the smallest kid in class, and constantly reminded of it, Kendrick knew from an early age that she would one day play in a world that was larger than life. By ten, she and her older brother would take marathon bus rides into Manhattan so she could audition for plays, memories she deeply cherishes. Her skin already thickened to rejection after fifteen rounds of schoolyard torture, Kendrick persevered, earning a Tony nomination for her precocious turn in *High Society*. Motion picture work beckoned and Kendrick went West, landing in Los Angeles, where she worked steadily enough to avoid the spate of odd jobs up-and-coming actors usually take. And then came the double whammy of a blockbuster vampire franchise and a quiet, brilliant film starring George Clooney. In person, Kendrick arrives in a black-and-white hoodie, listening to an iPod, not a trace of blush to be found on a face that is at once beautiful and absolutely approachable. In conversation, she is humble, self-deprecating, easy to laugh, and always kind. It's a mantra that's served her well, being good to people she doesn't know. It's that gratitude thing, that rule about treating people as you'd like to be treated, that maxim about us all being in this together. We're lucky Kendrick's in the same boat as the rest of us, even as one of Hollywood's fastest rising stars, and we don't mind saying so—even if it makes her blush.

SMALL FRY. Growing up always being the smallest kid in the class *did* have its advantages. It was usually silly stuff, like sometimes we'd line up by height, or I'd get to be on the top of a pyramid in gym class. When I was young and my family did spring cleaning they'd make a big deal out of how they couldn't get into small spaces, and they'd come to find me for specific chores instead of just having me clean my room. I remember feeling really needed. It was oddly one of the sweetest things they could have done.

BULLY BEATDOWN. While I wouldn't wish being teased on anyone, I think it eventually leads to a kind of solidarity in adult life. The few people I know who weren't picked on in school are people I find I can't relate to on much more than a surface level. There's a sensitivity that comes with feeling like an outsider at some point in your life. I'd rather be emotionally tuned in to other people than slightly more confident, because no one ever made fun of my hair.

GREYHOUND MEMORIES. The bus rides to Manhattan, where I was auditioning a lot, were mostly tedious, but it also meant uninterrupted time with my older brother who I secretly idolized. He'd sleep for a lot of it, but, at some point during the trip, he'd have to say something to me, which I would undoubtedly take as scripture and try to work into conversation with my friends the next day. I'm grateful for both my brother and the bus rides.

HIGH SOCIETY. I was twelve years old, doing my first big show, a musical adaptation of *The Philadelphia Story*. The actress who played my mother, a woman named Lisa Banes, used to whisper to me every night before we went on stage, "Let's go do a great big Broadway show." It's one of my favorite memories of doing the show, and I try to think about that when I'm down. I get to do the thing that I love and that makes me one of the most fortunate people on the planet.

THE FAIRER SEX. The movie, *The Women*, makes me absolutely glow. Is it perfect? No. But it's so much damn fun it doesn't matter. I fell in love with this film pretty young, and it might have been the first time I really loved one of the villains. Rosalind Russell plays Sylvia Fowler, a petty, catty gossip. You'd strangle her, but she's too much fun to watch. There's also not a male character to be found in a single frame of the film. I have no doubt that's part of what made it special for me as a little girl.

BAKE SOMEONE HAPPY. Baking is the perfect activity for me to shut off and quiet my mind. I have to focus on something very simple, but very precise for about an hour. I can't get in my own head about work, friends, family—just whether or not those egg whites are stiff enough yet. And then people treat you like a saint for doing it. It's genius.

HAVING A STROKE. At fifteen, I saw The Strokes on MTV at about 5 A.M., and I felt like I'd been hit by a ton of bricks. From then on,

I checked their website every day, which for the first month was just a "coming soon" page, just waiting for the tiniest update, or a new track or picture. I'm glad I got to have a little teenage Beatlemania moment. Unhealthy obsession is part of growing up, right? I also feel much more forgiving of the girls who cry over *Twilight*. Different kind of thing, sure, but I can look at them and think, "Yeah, I've been there."

EVERYONE LOVES GEORGE. The more I think about it, the more I think George Clooney is a mastermind. We're all just puppets. Some days on *Up in the Air*, I'd be so in my own head before work, and he'd be doing everything in his power to distract me. I used to think this was just George being the big kid that he is, but on the days when it really mattered, he'd be silent as the grave and unbelievably supportive. He'd never tell me, "Get out of your head, this scene's gonna suck if you overthink it." He'd just make sure I never could.

RED CARPETS AND YELLOW BRICK ROADS. I'm so, so glad that I prepared myself for Oscar nomination morning. The morning of the Golden Globe nominations was so strange. I was in a room full of strangers, getting ready to do an early morning show in New York. I knew that whatever happened with the Oscars, I wanted to be alone. I wanted to give myself a minute to process how I felt before I started to perform for other people. I was running at 5:30 A.M., before sunrise, in my neighborhood. My roommate text messaged me the news. When I think about everything that came after that, it's a blur—but I have that one moment, and it's crystal clear, and it doesn't belong to anyone but me.

Alicia Keys

on gratitude

"Breath and life, and the oppor-
tunity to try. If you have nothing
more, you always have that."

FIVE THOUSAND YEARS AGO, the Egyptians used the stars to orient the pyramids. In 2006, a superstar traveled to Egypt to reorient herself, after a stratospheric rise to pop music fame and a great personal loss. It was beneath Egypt's pyramids and stars, within the Red Sea and reading ancient history, that Alicia Keys—singer-songwriter, producer, actress, author, all by the age of thirty—rediscovered and fully embraced her own power. It was an odyssey in the classic sense, a journey to the heart, and the homeland, and one that has irreversibly transformed the artist. It is no coincidence that Keys's most recent album, *The Element of Freedom*, begins with Anaïs Nin's declaration of self: "And the day came when the risk to remain tight in a bud was more painful than the risk it took to blossom." Today, Keys is in full bloom, her life a sonnet of strength, solidarity, spirituality, and grace; her speaking voice an instrument of concord, her insights clearly gleaned at the water's edge. Born in 1981 to a single mother in Hell's Kitchen, Keys—née Alicia Augello-Cook—has always been a wunderkind, a piano prodigy at seven, a songwriter by thirteen, an early graduate and valedictorian of her performing arts high school, with a record deal in place before she could legally vote. Her music is piano-based, gospel-influenced, soul-inflected, with lyrics drenched in affirmation and empowerment, inspiration, and love. By twenty-one, she'd sold 12 million copies of her debut album, *Songs in A Minor*, which also collected five Grammys. Since then, Keys has not only sold an additional 18 million albums and won another mantelful of trophies, but she's also announced herself as a genuine artist, a force of nature, and someone we'll be listening to fifty years from now. Just to keep things interesting, Keys has also made occasional forays into big-screen acting, offering memorable turns in the bittersweet *The Secret Life of Bees* and, as a brassy hit woman, in the bad-ass *Smokin' Aces*. The Princess of Soul, as Keys is widely known, is also the cofounder and Global Ambassador of Keep a Child Alive, a nonprofit that provides medicine to families with HIV and AIDS in Africa. And it is this global activism, no doubt a part of her daily gratitude list, which creates the most harmony in her life. "Giving is the greatest way to touch a life—to know that you really *can* affect the world around you. It's so empowering," she says. "You help a cause and then you learn the names and then you see the faces and then you feel their spirits, and you're making a meaningful change in this lifetime, and it is extremely grounding and beautiful. It clears your perspective. It was something I was born to do—something that we're *all* born to do."

THE "KEYS" OF LIFE. My stage name has a lot of meanings for me. Originally, maybe it was just because I played piano, but now it has a lot to do with the way that keys open doors and the possibilities of what can be opened—what you can unlock, or even lock, inside of yourself. The more that I understand who I am, the more I understand the name that I chose for myself.

IT'S A STEVIE WONDER(FUL) WORLD. Stevie Wonder is the artist who first *really* moved me. He wrote these sublime songs that just touched my soul, and they were songs that I could learn to play because I played the piano, too. Those songs shifted my entire being—my spirit, my feelings, whatever I was going through. "As" is one of the greatest songs ever written. I still listen to it almost every day.

NOTE FOR NOTE. You never take life for granted. You never receive possibilities lightly. The opportunity is always there to help somebody. We all need help remaining in touch with our spirit and finding our own voice and locating inspiration, and it's a blessing to me that I've been able to do that for some people through my music. I've been able to move people through music, to help give a voice to some people, to help them find their place in a moment. Sometimes that's the best thing that music can do: give people a moment that lifts them, a moment that they can return to whenever they need to be given light. Every night before my band and I go onstage, we pray that the audience is allowed to feel light, to feel special, to feel something positive. It's beautiful to be able to walk onto a stage and do that. That's one of the greatest blessings in my life.

BRIGHT LIGHTS, BIG CITY. New York has made me so diverse. There are so many worlds that I could be a part of, or not be a part of, or that are already a part of me. I love the pulse of New York, the energy of it, the concreteness of it, the hardness of it, the way that you really have to push with it and shove with it to make it happen. The New York in me will never go away.

BIG GUNS AND HOT PANTS. *Smokin' Aces* was a chance to *release*— to get in touch with that crazy side of myself that we're always pushing to the bottom, saying, "Nah, I don't really feel like that." But yes, you do! Yes, you do feel angry and, yes, you do want to scream and, yes, you do want to control some things. It's okay to feel pissed off sometimes, and it's okay to need to punch through the glass. So carrying around those guns and wreaking some devastation in that movie was good therapy for me.

JUST DUET. I never thought of myself as a big collaborator, but then I look at the things I've done with Jack White and John Mayer and

Frank Sinatra and everyone, and I guess I am. The most amazing thing I've found is that these collaborators, when they're really great, they take me out of my comfort zone and into a whole other world that I know I wouldn't have accessed by myself. Our energies tend to go in one direction, unless we have the relationships that guide them into other directions. Great collaborations will take you into new territories. They will expand you. They will grow you. They will show you how capable you are of things you couldn't have imagined.

MORSELS OF MAGIC. Good food is an amazing blessing. Whenever you can sit down to a table and eat food that is extremely delicious, and you are surrounded by people you love, and you enjoy every flavor and every bite, it's, "Wow, life is good." You can't truly grow until you can fully appreciate a good meal.

THE BIG O. Oprah Winfrey showed me how business can be done in a positive way, with inspiration for all, that you don't have to tear people down to be who you are. You can be wealthy and rich on many levels—financially, spiritually, creatively—without taking a single thing away from anyone else. That it's really all about giving. I love that.

GIRL, INTERRUPTED. Stopping everything (in the summer of 2006) was a major turning point in my life. I realized that something just wasn't right in that moment, and I had to figure it out. I dropped everything in my life to go figure it out, *everything*—what caused it and what amount of life had I ignored or not dealt with from the past, from present relationships, family things I was going through, whatever it might have been. You can get into such a pattern, going from day to day to day, doing go, go, go, keeping yourself so busy, next thing, next thing, next thing, that you never stay long enough in the moment to be who you are. I'm grateful I recognized that moment in my life and took it.

THE HEART THAT FED. Visiting Egypt, I wanted to see the scope, to get the feel, to witness the temples and the tombs, to sail the Nile and swim in the Red Sea, to experience the history. The history and the sheer size of it all . . . even if you see the best *National Geographic* show of all time, you can't imagine how big things are in Egypt. They're *huge*! And it's all built one thing on top of another by the hands of human beings. That gave me an understanding of the things we can do as human beings. We are strong and powerful and historic and timeless and impactful. We can shape society. We can guide civilization. We are infinite possibility. And I am a part of that, and so are you.

PRANAYAMA. Breath and life, and the opportunity to try. We cannot take these things for granted. If you have nothing more, you always have that.

B. B. King
on gratitude

*"I'm proud of what I've got,
because I don't have what I don't
got, and I don't miss it either."*

IT'S NOT QUITE AFTER MIDNIGHT and you're calling
a Holiday Inn in the middle of nowhere, looking for one of the
greatest guitarists to ever live, who happens, at this moment,
to be kicking off his shoes after one of this year's 200-plus gigs,
waiting for a room service snack, gazing pensively out the window at the open highway below his sixth-floor room. It's late for
this eighty-five-year-old man who checks into hotels under the
name "Pump Davidson," a handle that once belonged to his great-
great-grandfather, a slave. "When you're young, it's hard to sing
the blues," said English singer-songwriter Nick Lowe. "Nobody
believes you." Unless you're B. B. King, that is, who might finally
not be young, but still approaches the blues with everything he's
got. King never had a worry pouring his guts out at any age into
the plaintive howls, ecstatic wails, and crossroad collisions of a
musical genre that speaks not only for *a* people, but, possibly, *all*

people. Born poor in Council Bluffs, Iowa, singing gospel tunes for his supper, music was in his blood. King always felt the calling, too, the inchoate, locomotive charge to play, to shred, to *be*. He bought his first guitar for four bits and fled to Memphis, where he connected with legendary players like Bukka White and T-Bone Walker, and the blues had recruited one of its greatest soldiers. By twenty-five, King was recording singles with Sam Phillips, who went on to discover Elvis Presley and launch Sun Records, and playing more than 300 gigs a year, a schedule King has maintained, with rare exception, into his eighties. In other words, for King, the thrill is definitely *not* gone. It's impossible to imagine music today without King's half-century of contributions, the coruscating vibrato, the exalting crescendos, the fluid string-bending, the intimate *dialogue* between the man and his instrument. *Rolling Stone* recently named him the number three guitarist of all time, behind only Jimi Hendrix and Duane Allman. In addition, he was honored with a Lifetime Achievement Grammy in 1987, and contemporary icons like U2 and Eric Clapton routinely bow to the King. After more than 15,000 shows spanning fifty years, King is every bit as much in love with the blues as he ever was, even if he's got more joy than he can pocket, no matter where he's been or where he's going.

BUSINESS SENSE. When I was in my early teens, I would sit on the street corners and I would play. I'd always start off playing gospel songs, which is what I really wanted to do. People would stop, congregate around me, listen, applaud, come over and pat me on the head, and tell me to keep it up. "You'll be good one day," they'd say. But they never tipped. (*laughs*) When I started playing blues, though, they always tipped—*always*. That's when I knew I wanted to play the blues.

GOOD HEALTH. I have played more than 15,000 shows in my lifetime. Up until recently, I played almost every night of every year. I'm eighty-five, but not dead. I've always been able to pick up that guitar and take the music to the people. I'm hoping it stays that way.

GOING HOME. I'm blessed with a job that I truly love and a job that allows me to see the faces of the people I work with: the audience, that is. Every show I play, it's like a homecoming. When you're doing that job, then you're sustained. It's a good feeling to know you're wanted by people. I never had a CD that sold 10 million copies. I've only had one record in my career played a lot on the radio, but I know when I come to town, my people will come and bring their love.

A GOOD ATTITUDE. When I was on the plantation growing up, I was proud I had overalls I could wear to church. Overalls are not the greatest garment a man can wear, but it covers your body, and I was proud to have them. It didn't bother me that I didn't have a $2,000 suit. I'm proud of what I've got, because I don't have what I don't got, and I don't miss it either.

WOMEN. Creation of the ladies is the greatest creation ever. I still think that today. Nothing better.

LUCILLE, THE GUITAR. That's the only girl I ever had who don't argue with me. She's my favorite.

THE MYSTERY OF CREATION. Playing, for me, is like expressing my nervous system. I feel what's going on and I play it. I'm no exception. I'm not special. I just play what I feel. When I'm playing the guitar, I try to pick out the notes that sound good to me, hoping they'll sound good to you. It's kind of like being a chef—I pick out the ingredients that'll taste good to me. Maybe you'll enjoy the meal, too.

THE KINDNESS OF STRANGERS. People have been good to me. I'm grateful to them. People all over the world. I've played in ninety countries around the world, and every one I've been to has given me a lot of love. People in music have been very good to me. No one's ever been hostile to me in this life, even in the days of segregation. I've been accepted.

GOD. I'm not the holiest person you've ever met, but I thank God for what I've had and what I've got. I'm grateful for it all—the windows, the light, the street, and the cars. I know I've been looked after in this life.

Sir Ben Kingsley
on gratitude

"Life is always richer when we're not playing who we are, but being who we are."

IN VARIOUS HINDU TEXTS, Krishna is a god-child, a prankster, a model lover, a divine hero, a supreme being. . . . It would only make sense that today's incarnation of Krishna, Sir Ben Kingsley, would be an actor, a hero of a thousand faces, and one of our very best. Born in 1943 to an Indian father and English mother, Krishna Pandit Bhanji (née Ben Kingsley, the pseudonym cribbed from a spice-trading grandfather known as "The Clove King") was probably always destined to celebrate make-believe and revel in adulation. He's always seen the world as magic, heard it as poetry, and felt it as metaphor. Today, in refined tones and deliberate meter, Kingsley examines every corner of life with intensity, hyperbole, and a fine artist's elegance; there is a reason Kingsley plays so many Shakespearean characters and Biblical figures, after all. To the Oscar-winning actor, all the world is, indeed, a stage, and has been since his father praised him for being "the Danny Kaye of our family," when he was but a small child. Kingsley, with his sharklike eyes, black, deep, and suddenly brilliant, and a thick, warm voice that turns electric very quickly, is a fearless actor, capable and eager to try anything at least once. Just ask the film maestros with whom he's collaborated: Spielberg (*Schindler's List*), Scorsese (*Shutter Island*), and Attenborough (*Gandhi*). He's played hit men and stoners, spiritual leaders and terrorists, doctors and depressives, frequently with a ferocity that lies tightly coiled until it explodes or implodes, usually with exhilarating results. Behind that brilliant serpentine quality, though, there also exists vulnerability, a wounded core or tender heart, a curiosity at the darkness of man or his world, a childlike sensitivity. It's what makes Kingsley—who was knighted by Queen Elizabeth II on New Year's Eve 2001—so damn good. A slow burn on screen, a poet in person, Kingsley is eager to count blessings, as perhaps befits an Indian god-child. These words pirouette from Kingsley's tongue in elegant strains, and he appreciates your listening just as much as you delight in his sage and theatrical declarations.

THE CALLING. I was at Stratford-Upon-Avon in my late teens, and I watched Sir Ian Holm play Richard III. I was so completely overwhelmed by his performance and the heat—it was midsummer, so ghastly hot, and I could only stand in the very back of the theater—that I passed out during the performance. I was revived by a kind usher from the theater and, exhilarated, watched the rest of the show at the end of which I declared to myself, rather histrionically, this is what I want to do and this is where I want to be. There was the germ of an actor well embedded in me previously, but this was really the catalyst. Two years later, I was a member of the Royal Shakespeare Company, walking the same boards as Sir Ian Holm, and working my way through the brilliant Shakespearean canon.

GREAT DIRECTORS. Archimedes once said, "Give me a place to stand and I'll move the world." Now, of course, he was talking about levers and fulcrums, but there have been people in my life and career who have given me astonishing places to stand and enormous responsibility and privilege and joy. Steven Spielberg is a shamanistic man among storytellers, and used his magic hand as a filmmaker to guide us all through the harrowing experience of making *Schindler's List*. But it was Dickie Attenborough to whom I owe the most enormous debt of gratitude. The opportunity he gave me (to star in *Gandhi*), and also the grace with which he guided me through that opportunity—that seemingly impossible task of playing that man's life—was extraordinary. Without ever making it apparent that I had never really done a film before, Dickie made it clear that he was utterly certain that I could do anything. He never saw any limits in me, and, therefore, I didn't feel I had any limits. I felt I could do anything.

FINDING ACCEPTANCE. My sister, Nina, says, "We must try in life to surround ourselves with people who have faith in us and with people with whom we can truly be ourselves." That is the trick. It really is. We are so easily seduced into being who we think people want us to be. As an actor, it's a trap I frequently fall into. I have this radar that reads a room and says, "Oh, they want me to be Danny Kaye." Wonderful, I can do that! But life is always richer when we're not playing who we are, but *being* who we are. It's essential, really, to find that company for ourselves. I believe I have.

WRITERS. I've worked with extraordinarily gifted writers, and I love exploring the musicality of their words. Steve Zaillian's script for *Schindler's List* was so brilliant, so poetic—almost blank verse, though beautifully disguised, running like a steel thread through the story. I get a real kick from finding the rhythm and the music in great writing. I love that. Even with lesser work, I can force a rhythm onto it until it sounds like music. (*laughs*) I think it's horribly unfair, by the way, for an actor to call someone a bad writer because these writers, they have put forth their best work, presumably, and said, "All right, now breathe life into this." Without their words, I am useless. So I am grateful to all writers.

BEING KNIGHTED. The English are very reticent of praise and enthusiasm. They don't bound up to you in the streets as they do in New

York or Los Angeles or Boston to say, "I love your work." They tend to look at the pavement or whisper to each other as you pass, and you wonder if they've ever seen anything you've done or ever been to a movie or whether you're something of a pest or an embarrassment to them. On the other end of the spectrum, there is this extraordinary thing that happens sometimes where they say, "Oh, it's okay. We have heard you. We've seen you," and they offer you the knighthood. Knighthood is this great redeeming gesture where they do, finally, admit to having seen you, and you say to yourself, "It is all okay. Here's the round of applause. Not bad. Now get back to work."

STORYTELLING. We are all spiritual creatures and live spiritual existences, however confused and disguised and sometimes downtrodden these lives might sometimes feel. But this is why we can be so profoundly moved by certain experiences and certain art, why millions of people can be moved by a sequence of notes written by Mozart or Beethoven or Elgar. Why does that series of notes move us? It resonates with something inside of us that is beyond explanation. It's ineffable. That is spirituality. That is what connects us all. That is why it is important to me to do what I do, to be a storyteller. Because telling stories heals us, doesn't it?

Dean Koontz
on gratitude

"We are all here for a reason, and, hopefully, that's part of what my books are about. When people feel that coming through, that's the best thing I could hope for."

IF WE ARE TO BELIEVE THAT IT'S NEVER TOO LATE to have a happy childhood, then we'd like to elect bestselling author Dean Koontz the president of our playground. After enduring a torturous upbringing—a horror show of extreme poverty and physical violence at the hands of an alcoholic father—a twenty-something Koontz simultaneously embraced Catholicism and his own powerful and prolific creativity to pen a virtually endless stream of pop fiction that has skated across genres to brisk sales. (Indeed, Koontz was once such a work horse at the typewriter that publishers insisted he use a virtual phone book of pseudonyms—from Richard Paige, Leonard Chris, Deanna Dwyer, Aaron Wolfe, David Axton, Brian Coffey, John Hill, Leigh Nichols, Owen West, and Anthony North—to keep from oversaturating the marketplace.) By the early 1980s, Koontz was a bona fide bestseller, topping the *New York Times* list nearly two dozen times, thanks to crackerjack suspense thrillers like *Whispers*, *Watchers*, *Odd Thomas*, and *Dark Rivers of the Heart*. Having sold nearly 400 million books, Koontz finds himself in the same commercial stratosphere as Stephen King, John Grisham, and J. K. Rowling. The secret to his success? "I have a low threshold for boredom, so when I sit down to write, I work really hard to keep myself entertained," he says. Enjoying a beachside lifestyle in Newport Beach, California, with his wife of more than four decades and their coterie of dogs, Koontz is always happy to count the blessings of his better-late-than-never happy childhood.

NEVER TOO LATE FOR A HAPPY CHILDHOOD. The childhood I had, it's not going to automatically fashion you into a Mother Teresa or an Albert Einstein, but it doesn't have to scar you either in any sort of deep way. You could probably say that I became a writer because of my childhood, but not so that I could analyze it—but so that I could *escape* it. But I was also always a pretty happy kid. I remember, in any hour of my life, looking around at the world and seeing beauty almost anywhere I looked. A lot of times I was looking in books, and that always pushed away the darkness for me. Books were an escape, but they were also a teaching mechanism for me: I saw in books that all families weren't the same as mine, and that was a good thing for me.

WORKING CLASS HERO. My wife and I once thought that if I could ever make $25,000 a year, reliably, that would be a remarkably successful writing career. I never saw *this* kind of success coming, and every day I wake up wondering, *How long can this last?*

ROMANCING THE ALPHABET. Funnily enough, in an age where so many people believe that language means nothing to what a book means or achieves, it really matters to my readers what the writing is like. They love the metaphor, the simile, the imagery, and I'm so grateful to have this beautiful language at my disposal. When I use language to full effect in my books, my readers tell me it creates a sense of the magicalness of the world. They love that the writing is cared for. So much of what's published today avoids that kind of care with the language. I've taken some heat for it. I've been told that you can't be a bestselling author with a vocabulary of more than 500 words. I think that's ridiculous. (*laughs*) My dog has a vocabulary of at least 300 words.

CLACKETY-CLACK, DON'T TALK BACK: THE PERFECT SOUNDTRACK. I wrote an entire novel, *Life Expectancy*, to Paul Simon's *Graceland*, and I've written two novels to the music of Israel Kamakawiwo'ole, this Hawaiian singer, who does this gorgeous medley of "Somewhere Over the Rainbow" and "What a Wonderful World." I've played that song fifty times in a row! I choose music that fits the mood of what I'm writing. I've written some novels to nothing but swing, others to the music of Chris Isaak. It works for me. It pushes the concerns of the world from my head and brings forward the story that I'm writing.

LOVE, ACTUALLY. You have to marry somebody with a sense of humor. You have to share a sense of the absurdity of life, and be able to laugh at things with your spouse. But perhaps the biggest thing is to remember you didn't marry this person for looks, though that may be part of it, but for something deeper inside of them that resonates for you. If you marry them for their soul, then you will always have respect for them, and that appreciation and respect will get you through even the tough times. When you approach a marriage like that, you are more than just a husband or a wife; you are a child of God, if you will.

THE LOVE THAT YOU MAKE. I occasionally get letters from people who only discovered my books recently, but then read thirty of them in six months so they get kind of saturated by the world view. They tell me that my books have changed their attitudes about life, that somehow my books helped them to see that life is more than hopeless. That always pleases me, because I believe life is meaningful and full of purpose. We only need to seek out that reason and pursue it. We are all here for a reason, and, hopefully, that's part of what my books are about. When people feel that coming through, that's the best thing I could hope for.

CHARACTERS IN SEARCH OF AN AUTHOR. I don't write with outlines. I do a totally organic kind of writing, so the characters take the story to places I never anticipated. They have a certain kind of free will, and I get amazed all the time by where these stories go and how these characters respond to certain situations. Of course, I'm controlling it to a degree, because I'm putting it on paper, but I'm not truly controlling it because these characters really are making their own choices. They do have free will, in the same way God gave us free will. I'm very grateful for this.

DOG DAY AFTERNOON. I have this affinity for dogs. I just love them. I'm so grateful they're here on this planet. And I'm told I write very movingly about dogs. I get thousands of letters from people every time I have a dog in one of my books.

John Krasinski
on gratitude

"A lot of these situations I'm in now in Hollywood, I find myself relying on my parent's son, rather than who I am as an actor."

IT'S SAID THAT EVERY GENERATION gets the hero it deserves. If this is also true for romantic leads, then the meteoric success of John Krasinski, *The Office*'s puckish, endlessly amiable male ingénue Jim Halpert, says a lot about the twenty-first century, and it's all good news. Quick-witted, well-read, handsome, and tall—but none of these qualities threateningly so—Krasinski loves his mom, cherishes his childhood friendships, appreciates all that he's got and has been given, favors canonized literature (especially that which has been adapted into feature films starring Gregory Peck), and is living, breathing evidence that nice guys do *not* always finish last. Which nice guys around the world love to hear, and so do moms or girls who will become moms. In this era of post-irony, post-cynicism, post-post-whatever, it's *safe* to love John Krasinski. John Krasinski, one of *People* magazine's Sexiest Men Alive in 2006, is 100 percent angst free. In fact, without being a frat boy or a vandal, he's also something of a *wisenheimer*, much like his *Office* counterpart, likely to hide your stapler inside a Jell-O mold or stash your wallet in the vending machine, maybe even send you a top-secret fax from Future You. He is a totem of good nature, playful ribbing, sincerity, and connectedness. Krasinski does not remind us of terrorist attacks, a crumbling economy, incurable diseases, or anyone who has ever lied to us — which is not to say Krasinski's unmoored from this reality. Personally, and in real life, he is deeply involved with a great many social and political causes and charities. He's starred in adventurous big-screen fare like *Leatherheads* and *Away We Go* and also wrote and directed the biting, poignantly deranged David Foster Wallace adaptation *Brief Interviews with Hideous Men*. Krasinski reminds us of the man we'd like to be (not the George Clooney vision of perfection men *wish* they could be) or the man we'd like to grow old with (neither a quarterback nor a nerd, but somehow *both*-ish). These are good things. These things matter. These things are real. It is not an insult to say that the world would be better off with more John Krasinskis. If he is, indeed, the new icon of manhood, the romantic lead this generation deserves, then it's just possible you, or someone you love, could be a John Krasinski, too. First clue? With a mix of absolute earnestness and wide-eyed wonder, say thank you for every moment of your life like it's the greatest gift you've ever been given. And mean it. Krasinski does.

A BLESSED BLOODLINE. I have the greatest parents in the game, to be honest. They were very keen on helping my siblings and I do what we wanted, encouraging us to make our own decisions, and identify what we believed in. They never wanted us to simply take things at face value — even *their* things. They wanted us to determine our own values and do our own work. I remember calling my mom in college when I was a junior, and I spent an hour just thanking her for all the things she did that definitely made me who I am today. In a lot of the situations I'm in now in Hollywood — which is very different from where I grew up — I find myself relying on my parent's son, rather than who I am as an actor.

REDHEADED STEPCHILD. I watched Conan O'Brien every single night in college, sacrificing lots of study time, probably, and then I got to work there as a script intern (in 2002), which was more like winning the lottery than anything else. I was starstruck every single day. Being there, being around that kind of creativity and drive and fun, was the first taste of the entertainment industry I had, and it set the bar high for me. Then, going back and being a guest on the show a few years later, was truly surreal. One of my favorite moments by far — being a guest on a show I had always religiously watched.

WHAT OTHERS SEE IN US. B. J. Novak (*Office* costar, producer, and writer) and I were friends in high school, and he asked me, senior year, if I wanted to play one of the leads in this parody that he'd written about the school. I remember being completely, totally in shock at what he saw in me that anyone would possibly want to see on stage. He said something, like, "Well, you're just a funny guy." I don't know how he even knew that. But I had such a great time doing that, and it inspired me to think about acting when I got to college.

OLD PALS. I can't describe how important my friends are to me, not only because I rely on them for inspiration and strength in good times and bad, but I would never be who I am without them. Each one of my friends has been so instrumental in opening up my mind to movies, books, plays, and new experiences. I didn't even know what an independent film was until friends started showing them to me in college. My friends have helped me become who I always wanted to be. They showed me the way.

I'M TOO SEXY. I am so grateful for that whole *People* magazine Sexiest Man thing. That was really cool, I've got to be honest. To this day, I'm fairly sure they made a mistake, but I'll take their mistake gladly. I think I'll have to go back and thank my parents for that. I think they did the dirty work there. I'm not sure it really has anything to do with me.

GEORGE CLOONEY. He has voraciousness for life that I've seen in very, very few people, not only in what he knows, thinks, and feels, but also in his follow through. He's not just an idealist and a dreamer, but he puts pen to paper, as they say. He really puts his neck on the block for many, many things, and that's the true definition of an artist. Whatever he does, he does it because he believes it's the right thing, the thing that will move people, not because he thinks it'll make him money or achieve status. Even by doing that, and taking those risks, I don't think I've ever heard one bad thing about him. Ever. He's so inspiring.

TO KILL A MOCKINGBIRD. This is the book that got me thinking on a whole other level. I read it in fifth or sixth grade and it was one of the first books that got me thinking outside the box, about bigger issues, thinking about what it means to have a voice and how to use it, and how you can connect with other people. I still find that book so inspirational. Everyone should read that book.

SURROUNDED BY GENIUS. I've been so lucky to have people jump in the trenches with me, all along the way. It's sort of astounding to me, how much people want me to succeed. Everybody I've ever worked with so far—all of the people on *The Office*, Robin Williams, George Clooney—they've all been so generous and supportive. I'm only a conglomerate of everybody I've ever worked with, stealing everything I can along the way.

Hugh Laurie
on gratitude

"At no point did I ever think, if I do this, it'll lead to that. But I've been to some good places."

SO THAT IT IS KNOWN FROM THE OUTSET, among the great and varied accomplishments of *House, M.D.* star Hugh Laurie is his rare ability to catch a ball on top of his cane. His colleagues believe he may be the only actor, living or dead, capable of doing so.

If mastering such parlor tricks, the fruit of spending desolate midnight hours on the working set of a hit television show, doesn't qualify Laurie as a Renaissance man, perhaps his astonishingly wide-ranging résumé will do the trick: class clown at Eton College, University of Cambridge graduate with a degree in archaeology and anthropology, British national rowing champion, English comedy phenomenon, bestselling novelist, distinguished musician, avid motorcycle enthusiast, critically acclaimed actor, and, according to a recent survey by Harris Interactive, one of America's top-five favorite TV personalities, thanks to his coal-and-sugar turn on Fox's *House*. Laurie—who is neither American (as his best-known character, Dr. Gregory House, is), nor in need of a cane (as Dr. House is, hence Laurie's proficiency at said trick)—is, he says, "occasionally perceived to be slightly taller in person than one expects."

If House makes his payments by savaging the landscape, the fifty-one-year-old Laurie always turns the scalpel inward; you'll never get the British actor to say a nice thing about himself. Ever. He is, however, fairly accomplished, and damned entertaining, at counting his own blessings, even if he comes to that practice through superstition and misplaced fear. In 2007, Laurie told the *Daily Telegraph*, "I don't believe in God, but I have this idea that if there were a God, or destiny of some kind looking down on us, that if he saw you taking anything for granted, he'd take it away." And so Laurie takes nothing for granted, except that he will receive it all backwards, a benefit—or curse—remaining from his days as a champion oarsman. "In rowing, you ride backwards, so you never know where you're going. It's always a surprise," Laurie says, wryly. "I should probably derive some positive life lesson from that, shouldn't I?"

THE SOUNDS OF SILENCE. The sound of my own voice is something I cannot survive. So I am grateful for silence, especially when I am alone with myself.

THE POWER OF MEMORY. In all senses, a memory is much more useful than intelligence. It's a much more serviceable quality to have. In the same way the ability to concentrate and persevere is more important than the ability to do the thing in the first place. One can be a great chess player, but if you can't keep going for eight hours, it avails you naught. Without memory, what are we? I may as well have been born this morning. At about nine o'clock. I had a rapid and loving upbringing. And I'm grateful for it.

LIFE IS BUT A DREAM. The funny thing is, when you look at other peoples' careers, it's very easy to see things as being constructed, planned, devised. You can see how they must have gotten from A to Z through a series of calculated decisions. In actual fact, I don't think that's true at all. I think everybody is sort of stumbling from place to place, from one thing to the next, and it only takes on a shape in retrospect: "Oh yes, I got here because I made that decision then and it led to this place and that decision." Which is how I went from wearing dresses to talking to animated mice to solving medical mysteries. At no point did I ever think, if I do this, it'll lead to that. But I've been to some good places.

STORMY WEATHER. I'm English; we never talk about anything. That's why we invented the weather. Weather keeps us from talking about anything meaningful or true. This may or may not be a good thing, and I may or may not be grateful for it.

ABOUT A GIRL. I think every actor always has that nagging doubt that he's going to be found out, that somebody, somewhere is going to stand up and blow a whistle and point a finger and say, 'You, not good enough, get off the playing field.' I think all actors have that in common. But I had this feeling that I could do this reasonably well, even as a child, being a class clown. This started out, all of it really, as a way of showing off for girls. It always does. If you can make a girl laugh, that's a start.

A MAN FOR NO SEASONS. What I feel like, I suppose, is a jack of all trades, master of none. I've always felt like I could turn my hand to a lot of things, but never excel at any of them. I do play the piano a bit, but I wish I could play it like Doctor John or Henry Butler. I act, but I wish I could act like Al Pacino. I do a bit of all these things. I'm just trying to dazzle you with quantity. I can't do anything well enough, so I'll do many things and hope that the quantity distracts you from the deficiencies. Maybe that's the plan. I'm grateful to be able to do *anything*, frankly.

SOULLESS BASTARD. I don't think I invest myself in the characters I play, actually, but in the ways the characters are presented — the energy and care that go into how something is done. I don't see that there's a lot of House in me, for example, or the other way around. House is (series creator) David Shore, really. But what I do is, I put all my heart and soul—if I had a soul, actually, which I don't; I travel light in that sense—into doing it right, getting the thing to play the way that it should. That's not to say that I'm losing myself in the character, but I do get lost in the intricacies of timing and tempo and connection. I'm rather obsessive that way.

SONGS IN THE KEY OF LIFE. I play (piano) only occasionally to the point of not at all at the moment. It just became so painful to appear unrehearsed, which was not merely an appearance but a fact. Professional musicians need to rehearse a lot, and amateur musicians need to rehearse an awful lot more. I just never had enough time to even be an amateur. I hated the feeling of getting to the end of a song and only then realizing what song it was and how it should go. I'd always get to the end of the song and then want to play it again immediately because I actually knew what song it was and what key it was in. That's no way to carry on. I'll be grateful to begin a song in the proper key one day.

WHAT HE SAID. Just bear in mind, I don't mean anything I say. Put that in italics at the bottom.

Stan Lee
on gratitude

"Other men watch the calendar or the clock for their golf game, but I truly enjoy going to the office because my work is like playing."

LET'S PUT THIS OUT THERE STRAIGHT AWAY: Stan Lee has a superpower. He cannot fly nor see through walls. He is incapable of catching bullets in his teeth or spinning webs, and he will also not live forever. Probably (though at eighty-eight, he's more prolific than he was at twenty-one, and makes Generation X look like Generation Zzzzzzzz). Lee's superpower is decidedly more subtle than those belonging to the expansive pantheon of gods, goddesses, mutants, monsters, superheroes, and über-villains—from *Iron Man* to *The Incredible Hulk*, *Spider-Man* to *Thor*, *X-Men* to *Fantastic Four*, *Green Goblin* to *Speedball Revenge Squad*—he cocreated during a storied, revolutionary tenure at Marvel Comics. To actually hear his superpower, though, you need to understand that Lee doesn't speak like you and me. Damn near a nonagenarian, Lee, nevertheless, brandishes a powerful baritone, affable and theatrical. It's a voice borrowed from a Roman orator, a Renaissance thespian, or a carnival barker—someone who absolutely must reach the cheap seats with his words of wisdom. (It's no secret that Lee is something of a ham; his cameo appearances in the Marvel-based feature films are small treasures of a Hitchcockian, *Where's Waldo?* kind.) On further reflection, it becomes apparent—as he greets you, "Is this really *you?* I want to make sure it's not an imposter!"— that he speaks in the burst balloons and bold-faced and teasing ellipses of comic book dialogue itself, each phrase exploding with import and destiny. But here's the thing with Lee: It's not some glib or showy affectation; it's a worldview. Lee's earned the right to tell his story however he wants. Born into poverty almost a century ago, Lee scrapped his way through a series of odd jobs—delivery boy, obituary writer, newspaper salesman—during the Great Depression, then worked his way into the comic book business. His first industry gig? Filling inkwells for established artists. By nineteen, the ambitious and charismatic Lee was named the unlikely interim editor at *Timely Comics*, wrote the popular Captain America title, and began dreaming up a roll call of comic book characters diverse in their powers, dramas, traumas, ethnicity, and needs for a really good psychologist. This depth and breadth of characterization set Lee's Marvel Comics apart from the work of rival companies during the tumultuous 1960s and 1970s, where the *Sturm und Drang* of Lee's heroes reflected the nation's own strife. If Marvel wasn't necessarily creating high art, it was certainly echoing and influencing pop culture in a fashion that resonates even today. Several of the past decade's highest-grossing films have been based on Marvel properties. (It's worth noting that in 2009 Disney purchased Marvel Entertainment in a $4 billion deal. As a former chairman of Marvel, stepping down in the late 1990s to create his own POW Entertainment, Lee will benefit from the arrangement.) As for that superpower? Here's Stan "the Man" Lee. Let him tell you. "Luck. Unfailing good luck. It's the one superpower I always wanted, and I'm pretty sure I got it."

ESCAPE FROM NEW YORK. My parents, my mother especially, encouraged me to read when I was very young. Those books opened up a world for me, took me other places. If not for those books, I was living a very tight little, narrow existence in a tiny apartment in the Bronx, New York, going to school two blocks away, playing with my friends in the neighborhood. This was the Great Depression. My father was, really, unemployed for most of the time I remember. We lived from hand to mouth. I think I might have been happier as a child if I didn't always hear, "But how will we pay the rent this month?" That was the one fear they had, constantly, month after month. But I'm grateful for the fact that, even though we didn't have very much, they were good parents. They bestowed a lot of love on me, and, later on, my kid brother. And what they couldn't give us one way, they gave to us in books and stories.

THE RUBAIYAT OF OMAR KHAYYAM. I love the beauty of the words, especially in the Edward FitzGerald translation, and I love the philosophy behind the poem.

There was a door to which I found no key

There was a veil past which I could not see

Some little talk a while of me and thee

There seemed—and then no more of thee and me.

The idea that life is so short . . . it's a magnificent poem, I think.

CAPTAIN AMERICA—FOR REAL. When World War II started, I enlisted in the Army and I was sent to the Signal Corps. They taught me to splice wires. My job was supposed to be to go overseas and get ahead of the infantry and make sure the telephone communications were okay. I was going to climb telegraph polls in war zones and do this work on the sly. It would have been kind of dangerous, but, in a crazy way, I was almost looking forward to it. It sounded so adventurous. It might have got me killed. But before I shipped out, someone found out I had written some comic books, and they transferred me to a branch of the service where I wrote training films and illustrated training manuals. I'm grateful I lived through that.

THE DEAD ZONE. There's nothing to be grateful for in writing about people who have died—especially when they haven't actually died yet. Making ends meet, I was writing newspaper obituaries for famous people on their way out, so that copy would be ready to go as soon as the celebrity did. That's how you know you're famous; your obit's been written before you're dead. It depressed the hell out of me, but I got paid to write. Incidentally, I hope my obituary's lying around somewhere.

FLY LIKE AN EGO. The one thing I always had was a lot of confidence. I would never write something and say, "Gee, I hope this is okay." I would usually say, "Gee, I hope people are smart enough to realize how great this is!" (*laughs*) I don't know where that confidence comes from. Please say that I laughed when I said that so I don't sound like the most conceited person on the planet.

MAN AT WORK, MAN AT PLAY. When I got out of the service, I went to work in comics, and I've been there ever since. So many of us work jobs we hate and can't wait until we're old enough to retire. Other men watch the calendar or the clock for their golf game, but I truly enjoy going to the office because my work is like playing. That's why I'm busier in my eighties than I was in my twenties.

THE CAPES BEHIND THE WORDS. I've been very lucky to have worked with some great, great artists (Jack Kirby, Steve Ditko, Bill Everett). They made these strips look so good that even if the writing wasn't that great, which it maybe sometimes wasn't, the books would interest a reader because the artwork was so spectacular.

THE ENTERTAINER. When I write something, if I'm enjoying the story, I'm happy with it. I'm not so unique. If I like it, other people probably will, too. You can't tell a great story if you're writing for *them;* you don't *know* them. You can only know yourself, so be true to that. Please yourself. Apparently, there are enough people on this planet as plain as me. I'm not so extraordinary, after all. Or we all are.

THE HULK. The big green guy is one of my favorites. I always loved the Boris Karloff movie of *Frankenstein,* but I felt the monster was the good guy. The bad guys were the idiots with torches, the mob, chasing him up and down the cliffs and hills. And then I thought of *Dr. Jekyll and Mr. Hyde.* Just a monster running around, page after page, would be dull, so why not have a man who turns into a monster and he can't control it. It's myth and old stories I loved, and things that interest me, and, I don't know, maybe there's something in there that makes sense about the way people really behave, too.

MAKING LOVE STAY. (Lee has been married to Joan Clayton Boocock for sixty-seven years.) There's no secret: I picked the right gal. She's my best friend. I'm crazy about her still. Forget about love. Love's important, but you have to really like the person. I got lucky.

THE TRADEMARK SHADES. I don't know what it is. I've always worn sunglasses. They're like my mask, I guess. (*laughs*) It was probably just some silly affectation. When I was very young and just starting off as a writer, I always lit a pipe and held it in my teeth as I wrote. I hated smoking a pipe, but I felt it made me look older and like a writer. I was eighteen. Sunglasses are better for your health.

Annie Leibovitz

on gratitude

"If you do something long enough, you know when something's good and when it's not. It's important to get to that place on your own."

HER PORTFOLIO IS AN AUTOBIOGRAPHY in a thousand faces: Mick Jagger, a phantasmic, after-hours Sikh; Whoopi Goldberg splashing, blissful, toddlerlike, captured in a giant bowl of the palest milk ever tugged from a beast; Dan Aykroyd and John Belushi, blue-faced and snarling, simultaneously violent, ironic, ridiculous, and sublime; John Lennon, a man stripped (literally) by love, hewing fetally to his paramour only five hours before death; Demi Moore, entirely nude, apparently moments from giving birth, hands draped protectively and provocatively across breasts and belly, angelic and brassy at once. Each face reveals Leibovitz herself, forty years into an astonishing career as celebrity portraitist, having crafted a body of work nonpareil that has rendered her as famous today as most of the people she's photographed. Her work is a breathtaking, utterly compelling study in pop iconography, and an extreme one at that—bold in color, rich in contrast, masterfully staged, frequently dreamlike, naturalism be damned. Leibovitz is the Joseph Campbell of click, the heroine of a thousand faces, capturing and manifesting her subjects completely, wholly, as never before, while alchemically—and probably in a way she would never confess—telling her own life story in vivid detail. Born in 1949, Leibovitz was a military brat, and moved all over the world with her father, who served in the Air Force during the crisis in Vietnam, and her mother, an art aficionado, who first put a camera in her daughter's hands. The adolescent Leibovitz shot her first photos in the Philippines, and she was immediately hooked. "Still photographs stop time," she says. "They have a whole other beat." She studied painting at San Francisco Art Institute and burrowed away in an Israeli kibbutz for two years during her late teens, before landing a plum gig with Jann Wenner and the newly formed *Rolling Stone*. For a decade, Leibovitz was the magazine's chief photographer, during which time she not only defined the look of the book, but of rock 'n' roll culture itself. Annie Leibovitz is the architect of our memory.

In the 1980s, Leibowitz's work became increasingly cinematic, her subjects more wide-ranging, and her reputation as one of the world's most gifted visual artists *ever* fairly unimpeachable. A major retrospective, of more than 200 pieces rendered in her book, *Annie Leibovitz: A Photographer's Life, 1990–2005*, has captivated tourists around the world since it opened in Brooklyn in 2006. The exhibit is a combination of Leibovitz's stunning portrait work and photos drawn from her private life: family members, her three young children, her longtime lover, the late author and essayist Susan Sontag. Leibovitz makes no separation between the photographs she was assigned and the ones she took in her so-called private life. "Either way, it's got to be an emotional thing if it's going to be any good," she says.

CHOOSING THE PATH. I was a young photographer starting out, and I loved the work I was seeing in magazines like *Life*, but I eventually had to come to terms with the fact that I was not a journalist. I was going to have a point of view. I was going to pick sides. That's just the truth about who I was. I finally had to say, I can't tamper and observe at the same time. You live a life or you watch somebody else live theirs. That's a critical decision for a photographer to make. It's good to know these things.

WALKING WITH GODS. Everyone knew who the Beatles were. It was more than just shooting another guy when you're shooting John Lennon. Even *I* knew that much, and I was just a dumb kid, twenty years old. (*laughs*) It was like photographing a God. I'm grateful for the people who had faith I could handle the job.

SOUNDTRACK OF MY LIFE. I've always loved music. I've always loved all *kinds* of music. But the music I grew up with, really, was folk music. It's funny, when I try to think of what's my favorite song; I really, really love "This Land Is Your Land." I segued into rock 'n' roll, like a lot of people my age, with the Beatles and then, of course, Motown—Diana Ross, the Supremes, Smokey Robinson. But I still get weak in the knees when I hear Bob Dylan.

THE ALLEYS OF EDEN. That time I did photograph Bob Dylan, we were in a recording studio, and I started taking his picture and he just said, "Come on, let's get out of here." We were down in West Hollywood, middle of nowhere. He made me, literally, walk around the block. It was a very surreal experience. He picked up a garden hose in this alley and just sat down in a stairwell. He just sat there and was doing his thing. It was the kind of photo session I would be afraid to suggest because it had no direction, it seemed. He just took over direction, and it was really great. He was playful. He was Bob Dylan. There were a lot of wonderful pictures from that shoot.

FALLING IN LOVE AGAIN. I think it helps if you actually *like* the person you're shooting. You watch them, you follow them, you see how they live their lives, you learn all you can. It's like falling in love with them—if "falling in love" is sort of a euphemism for "being obsessed with them." It's kind of crazy. It's kind of cuckoo. It's not the most healthy kind of relationship.

GETTING A LIFE. When I was younger, I was afraid to put the camera down. I was afraid I would miss a shot, and I was afraid of what I would do without the confidence the camera gave me. Eventually, I had to put the camera down so I could start developing a life. It was really an effort to put the camera down. I had to work at it. Once you have children, it's not so much of an effort. (*laughs*) You don't have time to pick up the camera. You find a way to be happy, just to be there. When you're younger, you use the camera to justify your existence. The camera can be a great friend—you get to go out with it, do things with it, it gets you into the cool places. It's a fantastic friend, but it's not real. Eventually, you need to make your way and relate to people. (*laughs*) I'm grateful that I did.

YOU CAN'T ALWAYS GET WHAT YOU WANT. When I was asked to shoot the Rolling Stones tour in 1971, I didn't love their music the way I loved Bob Dylan's music, or even the Beatles, but I *became* one of the biggest Stones fans you'll ever meet. I remember very well those days when everyone was comparing the bands. If you were a bad boy, you listened to the Stones. If you were a good boy, you'd listen to the Beatles. Time has proved both bands have their reasons for being. You can sing about the fool on the hill and not getting any satisfaction and be right both times. I got to shoot both bands.

MICK JAGGER. I spent five years with Mick and the Stones, basically, and the stuff I shot on tour with them, really, encompasses what it's like to be out with any band on any tour. It's a carnival, and a freak show, and a marathon, and the most beautiful thing in the world. Mick Jagger is the greatest artist and entertainer. Powerful. Impressive. Wouldn't trade it for the world.

NEVER A LAZY EYE. You don't ever stop seeing pictures. You always see them. That's part of having a trained eye—knowing what will fit in a rectangle or what will fit in a square. If you do something long enough, you know when something's good and when it's not. It's important to get to that place on your own—to know when you're hitting and missing—or people will spend all their time telling you, and they'll probably be wrong. One never stops seeing. It doesn't mean you're taking pictures all the time. But you're always seeing potential. *I* always do.

Elmore Leonard
on gratitude

"I've been very happy with my progress and always, since 1984, make the Times *bestseller list. I've got a tennis court and a swimming pool. I'm satisfied."*

PART OF BEING COOL IS EMBRACING PRAGMA-TISM, being humble, going toe to toe with your strengths and elbow to jugular with your weaknesses. They don't come much cooler than eighty-five-year-old novelist Elmore Leonard, whose lean prose, sinewy dialogue, and indelible characters have bushwhacked the bestseller lists for more than thirty years (*Out of Sight, Glitz, Get Shorty, Freaky Deaky*). When Dutch—as Leonard's been nicknamed for decades (the handle cribbed from a little-known, 1940s knuckleball pitcher for the Washington Senators)—says he can't be a literary writer because he "doesn't have that many words," and that he only writes because he really *loves* it, it's the truth. (Never mind that wordsmiths like Martin Amis—a longtime Leonard friend and acolyte, possessing, per-haps, one of the globe's most colossal vocabularies—swoon at every line that falls from the octogenarian's number-two pencil).

"I try to leave out the parts readers skip," Leonard said in 1983. And it's worked for Leonard, knowing what he's not and what he's got. Born during the Great Depression, raised middle class in Detroit, only nine-years old when legendary outlaws Bonnie and Clyde gunned their way into American folklore, Leonard always loved stories and storytelling. Post-college and post-Navy, Leonard worked as an ad agency copywriter, secretly penning short stories—westerns, primarily—during lunchtime and coffee breaks. By his mid-twenties, he'd sold thirty of them, mostly to pulp magazines. Before screeching into his thirties, he'd sold his first novel, *The Bounty Hunters*. Leonard's always been a professional, just being who he is. Today, the "Dickens of Detroit," as he's known, having lived in Michigan his entire life—"I'm too old to learn new streets in new towns," he says—is the model of cool: blue jeans, sneakers, a white button-down shirt, close-cropped hair, and round wire spectacles. Chances are good there's a can of cashews and a pack of menthol cigarettes nearby. His work blitzes the bestseller lists about once a year. He's prolific. Hollywood adores his work (Quentin Tarantino damn near owes Leonard his career). Behind the cool, Leonard is rich with gratitude and a gentle, puckish spirit. He's genuinely enchanted by the world, the one he inhabits, literally, and the fictional one he populates with con men, Shylocks, shady judges, and delirious Civil War re-enactors. It's there, behind that cool—not a pose or a calculation—just an authentic, subdued appreciation where wonder rules, chance reigns, and all we've got to do, really, is be who we are. Leonard calls it like we see it.

PERFECT TIMING. It took ten years to really get going and become recognized as a writer, but I'm grateful to be doing what I'm doing (and that I've sold just about everything I've written). I *had* a job. I always sold what I wrote. Writing's still the most satisfying thing I do.

OCTOGENERIAN IS NOT A FOUR-LETTER WORD. I'm eighty-five, and I'm still at it. I've got five children, thirteen grandchildren, three great-grandchildren, at least forty short stories and forty-three novels. You can't beat that.

BEDTIME STORIES. My sister used to read to me every night before I learned (to read) at school. She started out reading me a great series of books—this progression from nursery rhymes right up to "Beowulf" and popular stories, like *Treasure Island*. A good variety of literature. You learn how to tell stories by hearing them. I did anyway.

THE DRAMATIST RETIRES. In the fifth grade, I wrote a play inspired by *All Quiet on the Western Front*, which was serialized at that time in the *Detroit Times*. I had already seen the film. So I wrote a play about American soldiers in the trenches. We put it on at school, in the class-room, using the rows of desks as the barbed wire. Somebody crawls out and gets caught in the wire, and the hero's got to come save him. You know the story. There was one black kid in the school back then. I'd come from Memphis the year before, and didn't know any black kids, so I made him a German. I haven't written a play since. *You* should be grateful for that.

THE PRAGMATIC ARTIST. I wrote westerns during the '50s that sold well. Especially after I started doing research. But then the western vogue passed because everybody was watching them on television. (I didn't care for any of the shows because they all ended their first season with two guys facing down on some dusty Main Street, drawing their guns, which seldom, if ever, happened in that way.) So I switched to crime. I wanted to sell one and become popular. I don't have any feelings about literature. First of all, I don't write in a literary style. I don't have the words. Or inclination. I've been very happy with my progress and always, since 1984, make the *Times* bestseller list. I've got a tennis court and a swimming pool. I'm satisfied.

DETROIT. I've lived here most of my life, seventy-five years. I love the Tigers. I know the streets. It's a big city that got smaller. But it's home. Maybe thirty years ago I thought, "Maybe I'll move to San Francisco." But I never had a good enough reason to make the move. I'm satisfied in Detroit. When I would come to Hollywood, people from time to time would say, "You're from *Detroit*?" And they're all from somewhere else. I

don't think anybody's really from L.A., and I'd say, "Yeah, I like Detroit."
It's alive with all the major pro sports and all kinds of music.

WHEN WORK IS A PLEASURE. Writing should be satisfying. The
way I write, it is. It's a pleasure. I make it up as I go along. I'm not held
to an outline. I get the first hundred pages done, and I assume most of
the characters are already in it at that point and doing whatever they do,
and then I start thinking about the second act. How do I keep this going
with a couple of subplots? And then I finish it off. But I never know until
I reach, say, page 300 in my manuscript, how it's going to end. I never
know who might get killed or go to prison, or who might just walk away
and bug me after I finish the book.

MENTHOL CIGARETTES. I'm smoking one right now. Four butts
in my ashtray. I'm grateful for Virginia Slims. One of my characters in
Mr. Paradise, the girl, smoked Virginia Slims. She referred to them as
Slims. "I think I'm going to have a Slim," she'd say. And so then I started
smoking them. I think I found it kind of sexy that she did that. I liked that
girl a lot. She was a model.

FALLING IN LOVE AGAIN. I really do like my characters. We follow each other around. After spending so much time with them, I wonder
sometimes what they're doing now. After I finish a book, I'll wonder for
a couple of weeks, "Are they all right? Are they busy doing something?"
That's why I have picked up and used again some of the characters from
earlier books.

A ROSE BY ANY OTHER NAME. It was hard growing up as
Elmore. In grade school, everybody called me Elmer. I'd say, "My name's
not Elmer." But now it's fine. And it works great on the cover of a novel.
How many other Elmores do you know?

David Lynch

on gratitude

"Everything has consciousness, but the human being has the potential for unbounded, infinite consciousness. As your consciousness grows, you can understand human nature more. That's only a good thing."

THERE ARE NO FISH IN THE DAVID LYNCH *oeuvre*. Fear and desire? Yes. Pie and picket fences? Check. Locked boxes and Europeans in bunny suits? Oh, yeah, baby. Along with dwarves, dismemberment, rape, ridicule and ravishings, fugue states, black Joe, hot bods, and bothered dreams. Still, when Lynch discusses his work, which includes *Eraserhead*, *Blue Velvet*, *Twin Peaks*, and *Mulholland Drive* (recently named the best film of the decade by the L.A. Film Critics Association), he refers to them as "very big fish." A former Eagle Scout from small-town Montana, born in 1946, Lynch has practiced Transcendental Meditation for more than thirty years. He credits the brief, twice-daily practice with changing, if not *saving*, his life, and with richly informing his creative process. "Deep sea fishing" is, therefore, engaging in the creative process through meditation, opening the mind and heart to "concrete ideas that will hold lots of feelings and abstract things." This is how a severed ear on a perfectly coiffed lawn turns into the sexually charged, violence-soaked nightmare huffing and puffing of *Blue Velvet*. (Lynch discusses his "fishing expeditions" at greater, and greatly entertaining, length in the book, *Catching the Big Fish*. Who knew, for example, that Lynch's *Lost Highway* is really an O. J. Simpson biopic?)

Lynch also believes that Transcendental Meditation is the key to saving our planet. In 2005, the auteur established the David Lynch Foundation for Consciousness-Based Education and Peace with the goal of raising $7 billion, enough to facilitate TM training for anyone in the world who wants it. Lynch's belief, confirmed by a vast network of credible scientific and medical sources, is that a platoon of meditators simultaneously channeling their energies could actually affect peace, or dramatic positive change, on a regional, national, or even global level. This is why TM is being offered and implemented, with unanimously upbeat results, in penitentiaries, inner-city schools, and disaster-plagued cities across America and around the world. When asked if changing the world has always been his master plan, the filmmaker's exultant response is, "You got it, Buster!" The earnestness and affability, not to mention the brilliant intentions, are hard to resist. In person, Lynch is just so damned *nice*, an impeccable, polished gentleman, gently dragging on American Spirits, his hair perfectly shocked, a portrait of sincerity and kindness—and eccentricity—you'd like to know more closely. His speech is clipped, staccato, overly enunciated, creating its very own poetry. Lynch dreams like a Kafka hero, then tries to order that subconscious in a scientific, step-by-step lingo that sometimes feels like reading an Ikea instruction booklet. And then, usually, Lynch will make films in which the fever dreamer and the mad technician collide with dwarves, angels, nudity, and strobe lights. If Lynch is not saving the world, he's at least leaving his mark and, always, counting his blessings. Very big fish, indeed.

GETTING BETTER ALL THE TIME. I've been doing Transcendental Meditation for thirty-three years, and I wouldn't stop for anything. I've noticed that every day gets better and better. I'm just fired up, and I see ideas flowing more freely and way, way, way more happiness in the doing. It's just a brighter and brighter picture.

BYZANTINE BY NATURE. I believe that people know a lot more than they give themselves credit for. I love the idea that people can walk out of a film and think they have no idea what they've just seen and then find themselves talking about it with their friends and an hour later. In that talk, they're riddling out something they didn't know they knew, but now it's flowing. With things that are abstract, the interpretations vary wildly. And each one is valid. It would be just killing the whole thing if I were to turn cinema—which is its own language—back into words. I'm not that good with words. You work for three years in the language of cinema and then you're told, "Please, turn it all back into words for us." I'm grateful for the filmgoer who's got his own.

GRAY MATTER. Most of us only use 5 or 10 percent of our brain. When you are transcending, meditating with TM, you're having a holistic experience. You can hook yourself up to a machine and see this right now. Your brain can be fully engaged, and you're on your way, pal. That's something to be grateful for.

NO BERETS AND MOPEY FACES. A story will always have conflict—huge lows, huge highs, all kinds of shenanigans that human beings are up to. Stories are made of this. But the filmmaker doesn't need to suffer to show suffering. In fact, the more you're suffering, the less you can create. The tube of the flow of ideas gets squeezed shut by things like fear, anger, depression, sorrow, anxiety. It just squeezes shut. The happier I am, the better I create, the more I can actually understand human nature.

THE BANK OF LIFE. You come into life with a certain amount. The analogy is: You come into life with, say, $300. You can get along fine with $300, let's say. But someone comes along and gives you a way to tap into the unbounded treasury, and you can go there and get more and more and more. You can get that infinite amount. It's money in the bank. I think I'd be crazy not to go to that bank. So I go to that bank a lot between films, this bank of ideas, and meditation is my ATM card. It's just so perfect for the filmmaker, the painter, the artist, really for all walks of life. I'm catching big ideas — really big fish — in this way. You can, too.

LA VITA È BELLA. You know, there's a lot more to life than meets the eye. It's a great big beautiful world. Bliss is our nature. Life is beautiful. It's all there. It's all possible. I'm grateful for *that,* buster!

Seth MacFarlane
on gratitude

*"I'm grateful we get
away with as much as we do."*

COUNTLESS FUNNY MEN have said that the essence of
hilarity is timing. If timing is everything to comedy, then Seth
MacFarlane—the mild-mannered fiend behind television's
Family Guy, American Dad, The Cleveland Show, and the devilishly
hilarious web portal, *Seth MacFarlane's Cavalcade of Cartoon
Comedy*—has got to be the funniest bastard on earth. Segueing
almost seamlessly from preteen comic strip maestro to art school
golden boy to Hanna Barbera go-to guy to TV's youngest exec-
utive producer (age: twenty-three, show: *Family Guy*) to TV's
highest paid writer ever (that ka-ching you hear would be the
sound of MacFarlane's recent $100 million contract with Fox),
MacFarlane has enjoyed a fairly charmed career—and life.
There's that time he missed boarding one of the doomed flights
on September 11 by running thirty minutes late. Timing, man.
Timing. "I wish I could say my life and success have (been all

about) blood, sweat, and tears," says MacFarlane. "But truth is, a lot of it's been good luck and good timing." It would be easy to dismiss MacFarlane's comic bent as being juvenile or merely scatological, but that would be like saying *The Flintstones* is about dinosaurs or *The Simpsons* is about yellow people. It's true, MacFarlane's funny bone probably *is* stashed somewhere in his Fruit of the Looms, but shows like *Family Guy* are also hyper-intelligent social satires, mercilessly critiquing the American living room *in* the American living room, while also skewering hypocrisy, greed, and idiocy. MacFarlane's creations are boldly animated, a little gauche, lightning fast, in need of Ritalin perhaps—they give a Dutch rub to dusty storytelling devices like the flashback or stream of consciousness cutaways. Any single episode can be simultaneously brilliant, infuriating, knee-slapping, and jaw-dropping. Perched in a sprawling Beverly Hills home, his comedy central for apparently endless storms of inspiration, MacFarlane is smooth, polished, handsome, the kind of guy girls take home to meet the parents. He's also unafraid of failing, enjoying the nearly unprecedented on-air success of three TV series at once. Even if you may not love MacFarlane's creative oeuvre, he's grateful you noticed him at this particular moment in time.

EQUAL EXCHANGE. I think it's an even trade. Fox gave me $100 million, and I gave them my twenties. I think we're about even. I really do look at it in that way. I'm grateful we all agreed.

CAN'T BUY ME LAUGHS. Honestly, for me, whether it's $10,000 or $1 million, the question is always the same: How do you do the best work possible? On a day-to-day basis, the money hasn't really affected anything. It's still seventeen people sitting around in a room with no windows trying to find out what funny is. You'd never know any of us got a pay raise when we're sitting there suffering to be funny. But I *am* grateful for the money.

THE DRUNKEN CLAM. Peter Griffin (*Family Guy*) is every single big, fat, loud-mouthed guy that I knew, or my father knew, growing up in Connecticut. There's a certain breed back there that has a heart of gold but no self-editing mechanism. That combination makes for something kind of hilariously lovable. They don't know how horrifically offensive they are, and that makes them kind of forgivable. I'm grateful for all the people I grew up around, who are now on my show.

LOADED WEAPON. I still don't know if I'm funny. I operate, as a lot of comedy writers do, on insecurity in what I'm doing. There are negatives to that and positives to that. The positive is that if you're not sure you're good, you push yourself 100 times harder to be good. Sometimes you get there. Don't get me wrong: I'm confident in the shows and in the shows as comedy entities. But I'm still in the writer's room every day of the week pitching jokes I'm not sure have any merit to them. I'm always going for the kill without knowing if my gun is loaded.

SENSITIVITY TRAINING. Crossing the line of good taste is always debatable. We had a very controversial gag a while back, which Fox later cut. It's a Pat Tillman joke, the guy killed overseas by friendly fire. It's an Abbott and Costello routine, really, but it has to do with Tillman's killing. It got a huge laugh at the table. People there recognized we were treading into dangerous territory, but doing it with a certain amount of balance and awareness. Fox didn't see it that way. But in general, what's going too far? You just have to be sensible. If there's a plane crash or a fire that killed a whole bunch of people, we won't make a joke about it until . . . I don't know . . . at least three weeks later. I'm grateful we get away with as much as we do.

THE HORRORS OF HUXTABLE. I remember being a kid and watching *The Cosby Show* every week with my family. My parents were horrified by what wretched parents the Huxtables were. I asked them why, and they said, "Because they run their house like a military academy. They treat their kids like crap. There's no love." As far as the Griffins being emblematic of today's American family, I don't know. George Bush got elected twice. My guess is there are a lot of Peter Griffins out there. (*laughs*) And that means I've always got good material.

HANKS FOR THE MEMORIES. If you look at the film and television landscape, there are a lot more great dramatic actors then there are comedians, and there are a lot more great dramatic films than comedies. I was so depressed when Tom Hanks moved from comedy to drama. He was such a great comedian. Anyone could have done *Philadelphia*, but no one else could have made *The Money Pit* work. Thanks for nothing, Tom.

TIMING IS EVERYTHING. I've worked hard, no question, but my life and career have also been this hilariously, Mr. Magoo-like series of events. I walked right out of college and into the gig at Hanna-Barbera. Good timing. I learned what I needed to there, then this merger thing happened and I had the time to create *Family Guy*. Good timing. I did the *Family Guy* pilot which coincided with the success of *The Simpsons* and *King of the Hill*. Good timing. I was supposed to be on one of the planes that crashed September 11, but my travel agent screwed up the time. Good timing. I probably shouldn't even be here today, but I'm grateful that I am.

Malcolm McDowell

on gratitude

"I just happened to be in the right place at the right time an awful lot as a young lad."

VILLAINY COMES EASILY TO MALCOLM MCDOW-
ELL, onscreen at least. In a career that has spanned more than
three decades—spiked with memorable turns in films like *A
Clockwork Orange*, *If*, *O Lucky Man*, and *Gangster No. 1*—McDowell has set the screen ablaze with his elegant visage, piercing
eyes, shock of white hair, and perpetual sneer. Perhaps inspired
by his working-class origins in Leeds, England, McDowell, born
in 1943, is one of the hardest-working actors in film, television,
and theater, sometimes appearing in five or six projects a year.
It's true that McDowell is often—if not *usually*—better than the
movies he's in (yes, *Wing Commander*, we're looking at you), but
the man quite simply loves to work, each job an opportunity to
see a foreign land, shake new hands, or hone his chops. This is a
man who used to sell coffee door to door and tapped kegs in his
parents' pub after all. Wouldn't *you* have moved to Hawaii for a

year to reboot the *Fantasy Island* franchise for television? For years after his stratospheric ascent as a bad boy of cinema, a handle largely earned for his harrowing and blunt turn as the psychopathic Alex in Stanley Kubrick's *A Clockwork Orange*, McDowell struggled with typecasting. When Hollywood finally offered him a blockbuster pass with the well-received time-travel thriller *Time After Time*, the ripe opportunity was trampled to near-death by the somewhat-simultaneous release of porn maestro Larry Flynt's epic gag-and-jiggle film, *Caligula*. In subsequent years, McDowell has made peace with a world that wants him to be bad to the bone, and some of his recent performances are his best ever. (Yes, *I'll Sleep When I'm Dead*, we're looking at you.) McDowell is the ball of white heat you wished you could unsheathe more often, a truly volatile creature, a rampant Id with a demonic glare and impeccable tailoring. In person, though, McDowell—who lives in Ojai, California, which direc-tor Frank Capra once dubbed "Shangri-La" for its stunning vistas and pink sunsets—couldn't be more the gentleman, soft-spoken, with a rapier wit and an easy laugh. McDowell has lived a charmed life and is quick to say so, expressing a gratitude rarely displayed by those only capable of pure evil.

TURN TAIL. I would run, run, run from any of these guys I play. Run, rather than face any physical consequence. I'm a big coward, really. Well, I don't know if that's really true, but, anyway, I've never found myself in a position where I have to take a blow. And I'm grateful that I haven't.

KILLING KIRK. After I killed Kirk (in *Star Trek: Generations*), Wil-liam Shatner came running up to me and asked if he could put on his tape recorder. I asked, "Good Lord, no. Why?" He says, "Well, I'm writing a book, and I'd like to hear your views on what it's like to kill an Ameri-can icon." And I felt like asking, "Who are we talking about here?" But I didn't. I did say, "Well, I think half the audience is going to cheer me and half are going to hate me." He says, "What half is going to cheer you?" And I say, "Those poor people who've had it up to here with you for thirty fucking years!" He got a good laugh. Those are good days on the job.

UNCOMPROMISED POSITIONS. I refuse to kowtow to the audience. You must never look for any kind of sympathy. You have to show a character, especially characters like I so often play, with warts and all. You can look for no quarter. You can't be afraid of being hated. It's very important. Sounds so simple. But it's very important for an actor. Never worry about being liked. Consequently, I am very, very disliked. I'm okay with that.

THE SPOILS OF WAR. I've had enormous fun. There's wine, woman, and song enough for every group of actors that comes unsuspectingly along, and it was certainly there for me. Look, if I didn't have fun acting I don't suppose I would.

LUCKY BASTARD. I've been extremely fortunate, lucky. Luck plays a great part in it all. I just happened to be in the right place at the right time an awful lot as a young lad. That's how I met Lindsay Anderson and got cast in *If*, which is a great, great film. I think it's probably the best film—best film all around—that I've been in. And not many people even know it nowadays. But it's a watershed film in England. I think it's one of the best films that any actor could possibly hope to make his debut in. It's magnificent. Every frame is brilliant. How many actors can say they were in a film like that?

SOUVENIRS OF STANLEY. Kubrick kept all of the good props from *A Clockwork Orange*—the giant dildo, the cane, and what not, the bastard. You couldn't sneak anything out of there. I *did* keep a couple of the bowler hats. Incidentally, I just recently saw the film for the first time in many, many years. Mesmerizing. Astounding. I just went, "Oh my god, it hasn't dated one iota." I am just amazed at Stanley's work. It was a blessing—or pure luck—to be in that one. By the way, that's *two* perfect films I've been in.

1979. That was the year that both *Time After Time* and *Caligula* came out. I was in the top ten best films of the year, and the top ten worst films of the year on virtually every critic's list that December. *That* was fun.

JUST THE FACTS, MA'AM. I'm an actor. I like to think I can do anything. And I probably can.

JOURNEYMAN. Honestly, I've come to this conclusion: It's better to work. And even if it's only crap, then honestly, you're just always honing the craft. I think it's better to go out there and work. Work on your craft. Just do it. If it's shit, it's shit. But I'll always give it the best I can. I'll give a piece of shit the same Malcolm McDowell I'd give to Stanley Kubrick. It's all you can do, and I've done it all my life. To be able to work, that's a very real blessing.

Joel McHale

on gratitude

"I couldn't believe how blessed I was, and I thought, 'This is why I volunteered to be a snake thirty years ago!'"

SWIMMING FOR YEARS ON E! Entertainment Television's sarcasm-drenched clips show *The Soup* and enjoying a second season as big man on campus in NBC's hit comedy *Community*, Joel McHale is a very funny man. But he's also here to upset the cliché that comics are miserable, misanthropic drunks. You see, McHale is a nice guy. As funny as he is, and he *is* funny, McHale may be even nicer. Today, he's rounding the bend, looking to score, married for sixteen years, father to two young sons, buoyed by a razor-sharp wit, a tireless work ethic, a bountiful decency, and an absolute sincerity that is often at odds with his sarcastic onscreen personas. Born in 1971 and raised in Seattle, McHale also holds a giant secret. He's brilliant at the incredulous double takes and the sucker-punching comments of *The Soup* and at portraying the occasionally clueless, but charmingly quixotic thirtysomething community college student on the

NBC series, but the bulk of that work is reactionary. McHale is Fred Astaire-smooth with a one-liner, but he's also almost always playing off of his environment, be it talk-show clips or costars like Chevy Chase. Here's the secret: McHale is not only a great *re*actor, he's also a classically trained *actor*. He knows his way around the Bard and, probably, a pair of tights . . . and maybe a spear, too. But it also means he's more than just another funny guy, providing nuanced work in Steven Soderbergh's underrated *The Informant!* and gearing up for work in a number of other feature films. Through it all, McHale has operated on faith and gratitude, a trust that nice guys not only *can* finish first, but one day will.

THREE BROTHERS. It was great growing up with two brothers. We were all completely different, but we all got along, too—thank God. Today, one brother is an Episcopal priest and the other one works for a totally green garbage company that just started up in Seattle. When I put it like that, we sound like the set up to a "guy walks into a bar" joke. We all grew up beating the hell out of each other, which, I think, made us better people. Brothers are a blessing, man.

BIT BY THE BUG. My first play was in the first grade in Haddenfield, New Jersey. The whole school did this narrative rendition of "It's A Small World." I remember one of the teachers asking at a rehearsal, "Is there anyone here who can act like a snake being charmed out of a basket?" "Yep!" Like four of us walked up there, but I did a better job being a snake in a basket than the other three. I was, like, "All right, I got the snake role!" Then the teacher asked, "Can someone pantomime peeling a banana and eating it, like a monkey does?" And I was, like, "No problem!" I enjoyed every minute of being on stage. By seventh grade, I'd made up my mind: I'm going to keep doing this until someone says I have to get a real job. No one's said that yet.

BASIC MATH. When I auditioned for *The Soup*, I had been in L.A. for four years, and I had hopes that it would do one-twentieth for my career what it did for Greg Kinnear. I thought, "That would make me very happy." It's going pretty well.

KINGS OF KINGS. That Burger King commercial series in 2006 was awesome. It was right as the British *Office* was becoming a hit in America and the director wanted to sort of copy that style. He allowed us to improvise all over the place. There were a couple of ads where we never even showed nor mentioned the sandwich we were advertising. At one point, I remember asking, "Did we even *show* the burger?"

HAPPY WIFE, HAPPY LIFE. You have to choose to be with your partner every single day. Sometimes it's work. Sometimes it's what keeps you afloat and alive. But you have to make the choice every single day, no matter what kind of day it is. I don't know that there's any big secret to a happy marriage. I just know my wife is an enormous blessing in my life.

KOREAN BBQ. Thank God to the people of Korea for being hungry and figuring out how to feed themselves, because Korean BBQ is a revelation from God. I don't know why it's not the most popular food in America.

ABBEY ROAD. The second side of that album is one of the greatest achievements in modern music, in modern art. That *is* the album. It's been with me every step of my life.

THE INFORMANT. To be cast in a Steven Soderbergh film, to be given lines in multiple scenes, I felt like I had somehow tricked people, and it was all going to come falling apart. I think he is the best filmmaker—certainly the most provocative filmmaker—of our time. But he's also *nice*. He doesn't yell. No tension. He doesn't like long days. He just knows everything he needs to know. I couldn't believe how blessed I was, and I thought, "*This* is why I volunteered to be a snake thirty years ago! It really *is* a small world after all."

THE HEALING HEART. Our oldest son, Eddie, was born with two holes in his heart that he had to have repaired when he was two months old. That was, obviously, one of the hardest times we've ever been through, but as far as heart problems go, it was one of the easier surgeries to do. It's really the heart surgery you *want* to have. It was a rough couple months, but spending all of that time on the recovery floor with these other kids who were having valve transplants and multiple, massive surgeries, we realized very quickly how incredibly fortunate we were. Everyone kept saying, "Thank God he's so young; he'll never remember the trauma." And I was, like, "*Trauma*? I don't care. He'll be *alive!*" You got a little rough memory about some surgery you had? Beats being dead!

TIME MANAGEMENT. For a very long time, more than a decade, my life was all about working hard so that I could get the chance to act a little bit. About three years ago, that sort of flipped. I started doing some pilots. I picked up some little movie stuff. I got *Community*. And now I spend more time acting than I do *pursuing* acting, and I cannot believe that God would allow me to do all of this. I can't believe it. At some point, whenever this all ends, I'll look back at this as the time of my life.

Adam McKay
on gratitude

"I thank every audience I ever bombed in front of, because until you've really bombed you don't know how much you really want to do what you're doing."

IF YOU'RE WONDERING WHO TO THANK for the sight of Will Ferrell struggling through a psychotic episode on a speedway wearing only his butt huggers, wonder no more. That man is Adam McKay who also, incidentally, once faked his own suicide before a drop-jawed crowd of dozens. Don't worry, McKay survived (it was only a lookalike dummy that dropped four stories to the Chicago asphalt, part of the extreme comedy sports he played so passionately in college with his randy, rambunctious cohorts at Second City and Improv Olympics). Without McKay, the going concern about modern-day comedy wouldn't be "pretty or not?" but, "does it have a pulse?"—that's how completely the writer, producer, director McKay has captured the imagination of millions with his comic masterpieces. Usually centered around oddly principled boy-men on absurdly specific journeys of self-discovery, and starring Will Ferrell,

Anchorman, Talladega Nights, and *Step Brothers* are all classic *bildungsroman* with flatulence, and made with vaudeville-sharp timing, big movie stars, and unexpected twists of plot and tongue. (Unlike fellow comedy auteur Judd Apatow, whose onscreen surrogates are usually ashamed of the cheese they cut, McKay's anarchically egoistic characters own their bodily functions, and boldly.) Forty-two years ago, McKay was just another Philly kid growing up in a single parent household, too smart for his own good, restless, ready for something more. Forming a band of brothers with other fatherless sons in the neighborhood fed McKay's soul and, probably, fueled his affinity for potty humor. By college, McKay's social conscience was in full bloom, along with his pretensions to performance art and his uncanny way with a funny bone. McKay's early work was not only made up of pratfalls, double-entendre, and jokes about the private parts of Sasquatch, but was also politically fueled, socially aware, and *smart.* Stints with Second City and Improv Olympics led to his founding Upright Citizens Brigade, then to a jackpot gig in 1995 as head writer on *Saturday Night Live,* where he helped launch the careers of some of today's hottest comic talents. (Tina Fey anyone?) "SNL" connected McKay to Will Ferrell, who specialized in portraying tightly coiled characters capable of virtually anything. Onscreen, Ferrell was, and remains, a veritable Jack in the Box; crank him long enough, and you never know what will emerge: confetti, self-loathing, a non sequitur, a toddler's tantrum, or a mostly naked, speedway panic attack. McKay and Ferrell have teamed together for some of today's best comedic work, and it's all provided the impossibly generous McKay with more blessings than he could possibly count. "I mean seriously, we could do this for, like, six more hours," says McKay. "I'm not even kidding. I could never name all the people or things or experiences I'm grateful for."

MAMA MCKAY. She would read us storybooks from the time we were born, and add her own voices and jokes and be so playful. She would hand draw Valentine's cards for us. She always had a really creative spark. At the same time, she was also the mom on the block who, when there was a guy abusing dogs up the street, would get the petition going and go to the ASPCA to get the dogs taken away. She was a great role model for creativity and activism, and a single mom, too. I have the best mom in the world.

THE MINER STREET BROTHERHOOD. I grew up without a father, but I had this great group of friends on Miner Street, and we all looked out for each other—Travis Flynn, Steve Thumb, Jeff Pavolar, Pat Trainer. It was a big, circular street with a lot of kids, and pretty much every day we'd play hockey and football and baseball, all the time, for years and years we did this. We all played surrogate father to each other in some weird way. We'd pound on each other in football. One kid was always better at something, so we learned from him until it was our turn to teach the thing we were good at. I learned how to do a cut move in football on that street, and more things than I can remember. We did bad things too—throwing snowballs at cars and tomatoes at pedestrians and crank phone calls. On reflection, it's not even *remotely* different from what I do today.

THE MISSING LINK. Steve Landesberg was a comic in the '70s, who was on the TV show *Barney Miller.* I was in fourth grade watching Johnny Carson and Landesberg came on and did this stand-up routine. It was the first time I laughed really hard. The joke was: "You don't see a lot of Jews in the Midwest. What are you going to have? *Look, eetz a twistah!*" I remember *getting* that. I laughed really hard. I was hooked. It was a bridge moment between the joking that was always going on in our house and realizing other people were doing the same thing out *there*.

CLOSE ENCOUNTERS. When you study with Del Close (Second City and Improv Olympics veteran), you're studying with, probably, the greatest comedy teacher of all time. His rules were radical and radically different from what anyone else was teaching at the time. He was from the buttoned-down 1950s generation—the Elaine May and Mike Nichols era. They preached being politically aware, reading literature, the responsibility of the performer to get information and find out things someone who's working sixty hours a week as a plumber doesn't have time to get. "Treat your audience like poets and geniuses, and that's how they'll behave," is something Del taught us. "Play at the top of your intelligence." If you're playing a dumb guy, make *brilliantly* dumb choices. It wasn't just going out for laughs; it was a mission.

WORKING CLASS HEROES. I'm grateful for all of the people in the past thousands of years who died, were beaten, or were arrested for our rights and freedoms—the union people in the early twentieth century who decided they wanted a weekend or a forty-hour work week or didn't want nine-year-olds to work full-time jobs and get abused. We so take that for granted now, because we forget how much they sacrificed for the lives we live today.

HOW TO DISMANTLE A COMEDIC BOMB. When I started doing stand-up comedy in Philadelphia, I was so nervous I could barely take the mic off the stand. I could barely half mumble my jokes. One night, this guy in the audience was flicking bottle caps at me. The whole set. That is a *rough* gig. You really feel like an animal in a cage at that point. But I stayed with it. I made it through that night, that guy and all his bottle caps, and I thank him. I thank him very much. In fact, I thank every audience I ever bombed in front of, because until you've really bombed you don't know how much you really want to do what you're doing. If you can bomb to death one night, but still need to go out and do it again, you probably should. You have to bomb in order to get better. I bombed *a lot*.

THE LIST IS LIFE. When I wrote for *Saturday Night Live*, it was a show every week. We had to come up with new stuff all the time. So I had this ritual: Every Sunday night, before the Monday pitch meeting, I would make myself write down twenty ideas. No matter how terrible they were. Always twenty. Even if nineteen really sucked, there's always one that's at least one-quarter okay. Del Close trained us to know that there's no such thing as a bad idea. If the idea is there, then there's *something* there of value. It's a matter of digging it out and finding it.

THE WILL AND THE WAY. This is one of the great collaborations of my life. Will Ferrell has got such a healthy ego, and he's such a decent guy. He really does his work because he loves it, which is why I do it. He's not doing this to make money or to be famous. He does this because he loves to laugh. And we happen to find the same things funny. I mean, I lucked out. I found the perfect relationship.

THE BOYS OF SUMMER. The '78 Red Sox, Fred Lynn, and Jim Rice. I used to *love* the Red Sox when I was a kid, and those two guys were just murderers. They'd knock the crap out of the ball, and that was so much fun to watch. That was *years* of enjoyment.

THE MERRY MUTANTS. When we were kids, my buddy, Jeff Pavolar, and I would get on our bikes and ride, conservatively, ten or twelve miles off of a highway, all the way to the next town over because our town didn't have comic books, to get the new "X-Men" on the day it would come out. We'd each buy a copy of the comic, then sit out in front of the comics store, right on the curb because we couldn't wait to read the story, usually written by this guy Chris Claremont. This was Wolverine time, man. After we read the comic book, we'd roll it up and put it in our back pockets, ruining its value of course, and ride back home. The whole thing would take, like two and a half hours, but those are good hours in a young man's life.

PAPA MICHAELS. I have to thank Lorne Michaels on numerous levels: 1) He created *Saturday Night Live,* which, when I was a kid, changed my perspective and taught me so much about what was funny; 2) Double thank you to Lorne Michaels, because he gave me my first legit gig when he hired me as a writer on *Saturday Night Live*; 3) Then another thank you to Lorne Michaels because he was the guy who let me direct for the first time. He gave me some budget money to go and experiment and make some short films and learn how to direct; and then 4) He gave me enough shit to appreciate shittier jobs down the road and to make them look comparatively easy. I'm thankful for all of that.

GOD. I'd like to thank God for everything. Amen.

Brad Meltzer
on gratitude

"You can look at your life and say, 'I'm so glad that this wonderful thing happened,' but we rarely do that with sad things. Maybe we should."

BRAD MELTZER MAY LOOK LIKE A CLARK KENT, timid, bespectacled, slight of frame, unassuming, but make no mistake: He *is* a Superman. It's not that his bared chest can deflect buckshot, or his furrowed brow can detect the cut and color of your skivvies. It's not even that, at forty, he's already penned a shelf full of crackerjack bestsellers that read like Dan Brown by way of Michael Chabon (you're a Superman yourself if you can put down Meltzer's *The Book of Fate* or *The First Counsel*), created a critically lauded television series (the short-lived *Jack & Bobby*), contributed essential, much-loved chapters to the long-running saga of comic book legends Justice League of America, or helped Homeland Security's Analytic Red Cell program prevent terrorism by imagining unconventional attack scenarios. What makes Meltzer, who lives in Florida with his high school sweetheart and their three children, such a Superman is his faith in values once embraced as all-American: integrity, kindness, generosity, compassion, the importance of hard work, and the possibility of reinvention. It takes a superheroic frame of mind these days to believe that ordinary people can change the world, and yet that's *exactly* what all of Meltzer's novels are about and, also, the name of the charity organization he founded in 2008. On the one hand, we need superheroes because we need to believe in something (and, as Hollywood tells it, we like to see endless bytes of computer animation and ginormous explosions). On the other hand, we need superheroes because they believe in *us*. The only thing separating Batman from the rest of Gotham City in the recently reimagined Batman film franchise is the mask and cape. Beyond that, Gothamites are all faced with the same heady moral dilemmas, the same yearning for redemption, the same do-or-die scenarios. Meltzer knows this, embraces this, and lives his life accordingly, as if every choice he makes is one that impacts the rest of the world for better or worse. Consequently, you'll rarely meet a kinder man. If your car's broken down along Highway 95, it's quite possibly Meltzer who will give you a lift, or maybe the shirt off his back. If all of this sounds like the resume for the most boring Sunday school teacher in the world, just pick up one of Meltzer's novels. They're breathtaking puzzle boxes of political intrigue, conspiracy theory, and labyrinthine relationships penned by a virtuoso. That the moral of the stories—*embrace your power as the best person you can be*—is as old as time doesn't mean Meltzer is Kryptonite to your good time. Indeed, Meltzer may be the most fun you ever had with a book.

HOUSE OF BOOKS. When I was little, we didn't have money, but we did have a library card. I remember getting the card. I remember signing my name on it. I remember going to the library and the smell of the Mylar that was wrapped on all of the books. There was a little section in the middle of the library—almost an island—that was dedicated to kids' books. That was our little island. It was where I first fell in love with the printed page. I owe my grandmother forever for taking me there, and every librarian in the world, too.

CHICKS WITH BRICKS COME. *Fox in Socks* has always been my favorite kids' book. I love it because it's a tongue twister. It didn't have the moral lesson—the fear of mom like *Cat in the Hat,* no narrative like some of the other Dr. Seuss books—but, boy, was it fun. Every time it was read to me, I'd be laughing my head off at those tongue twisters. That was it for me.

A ROYAL GAME OF INDIA. When I was little, we'd go to camp, and we only had one game. We had Parcheesi. All the other kids had Monopoly and Mousetrap and checkers and chess. We had the one game, and boy, we played it like it was nobody's business. It'd be very easy to say Parcheesi was my quest for home, and that's all I really wanted as a kid moving around a lot, but I think it was just a game I really loved—a game I played with my mom and my dad and my sister. It's what I remember best from my childhood, and I'm grateful for it.

BLUBBERING BOY. When I was a kid, I loved Judy Blume and Agatha Christie. That was it for me. Growing up, I was, basically, a thirteen-year old girl.

MY TIME IS A PIECE OF WAX. We were watching that show *Modern Family* a couple of weeks ago, and one of the characters said, "There's a point in time where no one wants to be different, and then, suddenly, there's a point in time where *everyone* wants to be different. Those of us who *are* different, we actually get a head start." That might have been true of me. There was a little bit of a difference in me as a kid, and I love that—even if those things made me a "loser" at the time.

IMPOSSIBLE DREAMERS. Mr. Rogers and Jim Henson were unapologetic idealists, and they're two of my greatest heroes. One of them went on TV every day for the sole reason of telling kids that they're special. And Jim Henson was at the top of the game—the Steven Spielberg of his milieu. He could've done anything he wanted, and he devoted his life to public television for children. I love that. People wonder if it matters, and it *does.*

GOTHAM'S FINEST. I'll never be Superman. I'll never be able to fly. I'll never lift a car over my head. I'll never have X-ray vision or come from another planet. Even on my best day. But Batman is just a stubborn guy who trained himself. I can be *that* guy. I'm not going to put on a cape or wear underwear on the outside of my pants, but the idea that I can be *that*, it's pretty cool.

THE GOOD NEWS ABOUT BAD NEWS. You can look at your life and say, "I'm so glad that this wonderful thing happened," but we rarely do that with sad things. Maybe we should. My first book got twenty-four rejection letters. There were only twenty publishers at the time, which means that some people wrote me twice to make sure I got the point. But I still believe to this day that if that book had sold and it had been a home run right off the bat, I would never have appreciated anything else I have today. I'm grateful it took some time for me to find success.

GARBAGE PAIL KID. It was one of the worst professional days I've ever had. My publisher was shutting down, and they, basically, said, "We can't do your book, and we're not sure if anyone else will take you." It was one of those terrifying moments. It felt like everything I'd worked for was disappearing in front of my face. I thought my career was over. I called my mother and was asking her, "What if it all falls apart? What if I'm finished?" And she said, "I'd love you if you were a garbage man." Every day to this day, every single time I sit down to write, I say those words to myself.

NUMBER ONE WITH A BULLET. The first person I called when we reached number one for the first time was my mother. I told my mom the news, and she started hysterically crying. When you hear your mom cry, often times it makes you well up, too. And then I start getting nervous, because my mom *must* be driving somewhere, and so she's going to crash the car while she's driving, obviously. So I ask her, "Mom, where are you?" And she says, "I'm in Marshalls." We're at the number-one spot on the *New York Times* bestseller list, and my mom's shopping for a $4 blouse at Marshalls. To this day, it's the greatest lesson my mother's ever given me, which is to never, ever, ever, ever, ever, *ever* change for anyone. It put everything in that moment into perspective. I remember when we shopped at Marshalls because we couldn't afford to shop anywhere else, and I love the fact that my mother *always* shopped at Marshalls—even when she didn't have to.

THE WOODMAN COMETH. I was at a book signing in New York many years ago, and a woman handed me a business card that said, "Be a part of cinematic history. The new Woody Allen movie is looking for extras, and we want you." I thought, "This is my moment. I've waited my entire life for this." *Annie Hall* is still my favorite movie of all time. I spent two days on the set of Woody Allen's *Celebrity*, hanging out with the authors Erica Jong and Lorenzo Carcaterra trying to figure out why Woody Allen had chosen *us* of all people. We knew the stories about how Woody Allen handpicks his extras and how he controls every aspect of his productions, and we couldn't figure out why he'd chosen us. We were utterly amazed, and, for me, this was a real dream come true, being directed by Woody Allen, one of my all-time heroes. We finally figured it out: all three of us happened to be signing books at the same Barnes & Noble that week. It had nothing to do with being anything more than a dummy in the right place at the right time. Sometimes life is like that, and I'm okay with that.

NOTHING'S LOST, ALL IS GAIN. When I was researching my novel, *Book of Fate*, former President George H. W. Bush invited me to Houston. I'll never forget him telling me about his last time on Air Force One. He said, the plane touches down and you say goodbye to the pilot, and you say goodbye to the people on the plane, and you pick up the phone, and you say goodbye to the White House operators, and all the people who served you, and you come down the stairs into your hometown, and there's no big, giant parade waiting for you. You're not the president anymore. It's just a small group of reporters waiting for you. That's about it. So President Bush came down the stairs and a reporter shouted out, "How does it feel to be back, sir?" He put on a big smile and said, "It feels great!" And he tried not to think about what the real, truthful answer was. I love that story. We all have those moments where we could announce our heartbreak or sadness, but where it serves the world—and ourselves—to put on a stronger face than that.

PUPPY LOVE. There was a point in time where if you put the words "high school sweetheart" into Google, my website was the first thing that came up. I think it's because of a blog I wrote saying how thankful I was for marrying my high school sweetheart. I would get inundated with e-mails from high school sweethearts from all over America, getting ready to graduate or go off to college. They all wanted to know, "Will it work?" My honest belief was—and is—"No, it probably won't." I don't think that's a bad thing; it's just reality. I think to myself every day how amazing it is that, of all the ways and directions my high school sweetheart and I *could have* grown, we actually grew in the same direction. My wife's love is one of the most important constants in my life. She knows me before I ever tried anything. When I first decided I was going to be a writer, we were sitting in a restaurant together. The job I was working wasn't going very well. I didn't know what I was going to do. So I told her I'd like to take a year to write a novel. And my wife did the most important thing a wife can do for her husband when he's got a wild idea: *She didn't laugh*. You have to appreciate support like that.

ORDINARY PEOPLE CHANGE THE WORLD. Some writers spend their entire lives knowing exactly what the theme or themes of their books are going to be. It took me six novels before I realized mine. I finally realized I'm always writing about the same thing: this core belief that ordinary people change the world. I don't care where you went to school. I don't care how much money you make. What I care about is regular people. *That's* how the world changes. We launched this website (*www.ordinarypeoplechangetheworld.com*) to remind people that the best change in the world comes from regular, ordinary, boring people. There's a line in my new novel that says: "History doesn't choose individuals. History chooses everyone every single day. The only question is: Do you hear the call." I think you have to stop and listen to that call sometimes.

Yao Ming
on gratitude

"In that moment, I felt like we were a part of the people, a part of the country, we are one. Walking into that stadium, we were finally accepted."

YAO MING IS LARGER THAN LIFE. But not only because, at seven feet five inches, he is a human skyscraper or because he's been China's richest man for nearly a decade running or because he is one of the greatest centers basketball has ever seen, which is partially because of the former and the cause of the latter. The thirty-year-old Yao, recruited by the Houston Rockets in 2002, and also a five-time NBA All Star, was essentially born into basketball. As the only son of two professional basketball players in China, he was raised in and around the game, and his body was seemingly crafted for excellence within its rule book and arenas. Yao is a record-setter and a record-smasher, the Rockets' powerful engine who could (and does), drive the team repeatedly to post-season play. But Yao, who was five feet five inches at the age of ten, is more than a Chinese legend or an American superstar, more than a Shanghai boy made good or the tallest man in

Texas. His genius for the game is well known, but Yao is also a devoted philanthropist. The sports star has raised hundreds of thousands of dollars for underprivileged children in China through the Yao Ming Foundation, providing aid for victims of the 2008 Sichuan earthquake, and even offering a financial boost to the cash-strapped Shanghai Sharks, the club team he played on as a teenager. Yao is a true believer, a gentleman and a gentle man who straddles the worlds of China (where he still plays occasionally) and America (where he is widely considered one of the best players in the game). Yao Ming is larger than life because, like all great athletes, he shows us what we wish we could be and then, like only he could, shows us exactly how it's done.

RISING SUN. Carrying the flag of China into Beijing National Stadium during the 2008 Olympics was the biggest moment of my life. All the training I'd done, all the preparation I'd done, all of the work in my life, it was for that moment, to have the Olympics in my homeland. And in that moment, I felt that I was not a kid anymore. None of China's athletes were kids anymore. Usually, the athlete in China is treated like a kid because we do not really connect with people. We are always taught to train and to get better and get more goals and win more games, right? But in that moment, I felt like we were a part of the people, a part of the country, we were one. Walking into that stadium, we were finally accepted.

SLAM-DUNK BABY. My parents are former professional basketball players. They had very successful careers before I was born, but in the '70s in China, the professional athlete didn't make enough money for an entire lifetime. When their careers ended, they had to find new jobs just to make money to survive. They had to start over, no matter how successful they were. I'm glad that's different today.

DRILL TO THRILL. When I was fourteen, I was part of the Shanghai Sharks youth basketball training camp. We worked out ten or twelve hours a day, six days a week. There were fifteen or sixteen of us in the camp, and only half of us would make it all the way through the summer.

Kids don't need that much training for playing basketball. I realize now it wasn't about physical training; all of the hard work is *mental* training. It's about what's going on in your head. The practicing may have made my basketball skills better, but I know it made me tougher in other ways.

THE PASSING LANE. I play a team sport, so teamwork is very important to me — in the game and in my life. The team sport is not only about how good you are, it's about how well you can play with the other people on your team. How well can you read people? How well can you hear people? How well can you connect with people? That's not about basketball skills; that's about human interaction. It's chemistry, whether there's a ball involved or not. I have a good team in my life.

YEAR OF THE YAO. When I think back on my childhood in China, it's the Chinese New Year celebration that I love the most. It's the biggest holiday in my country. It's a family time — my parents, my grandparents, aunts, uncles, and cousins, we would all be together. We'd have a big dinner and celebrate, but, mostly, we would just be together, and I always loved that. It's like Thanksgiving in America.

UP IN THE AIR. Being seven feet five inches tall, I probably have more fresh air than anyone else on the planet. Being higher is better for air quality, right? When I was little, I wished I could grow very tall like my father. When I was twenty, I was taller than my father and became worried about being that tall. I did not want people looking at me like I was strange. Part of my success in basketball is because of my size, so I have to be grateful for it. I cannot complain about being so big because it is who I am, and it has allowed me to do what I love to do.

THE UNKNOWN SOLDIER. I play World of Warcraft on the computer a lot because I can be a normal guy inside of the game. Nobody realizes who I am. I am anonymous. I can act like a normal person and talk like a normal person — maybe even say some bad words. (Not that many, because I'm still me. The things I would not do in the real world I would not do in the game, either.) But most importantly, time inside that game is time where I don't have to be tall or be a basketball player. I can connect to other people normally and play in a fake war. I am grateful for that.

BILLY PILGRIM'S FAST BREAK. Someone once asked me, "If you could go back in time and tell your fourteen-year-old self something about your life today, what would you do? Would you change any of your mistakes or challenges?" I would not change anything. All of the challenges have made me who I am. You have to live your life as it happens, good experiences and bad. In fact, the greatest opportunity you have is to learn from your opponent. You learn the most from the moments that are against you. All of the challenges I have had in my life, I appreciate them.

Steve Nash

on gratitude

"It feels compelling to me— natural—to get involved in help- ing improve the lives of others. It's important, and it's really fun."

THE WORD "ASSIST" MEANS A LOT OF THINGS in the world of Steve Nash. While most twenty-first century point guards are better known for scoring big than sharing glory, the Canadian import, the big gun of the Phoenix Suns, born in 1974, plays old school ball, moving mindfully around the court, employ- ing uncommonly equal game play that spreads the wealth and usually wins the game. For Nash, it's the mission, not the moment; the big picture of the game and not the instant gratification of the highlight reel. Therefore, for many of his fourteen seasons, Nash has led the NBA in assists—smart, generous moves that allow others to be more than they might be otherwise. Nash does the same thing off the court, heading the Steve Nash Founda- tion, a nonprofit that works internationally on behalf of at-risk and underprivileged youth. Born in South Africa, Nash credits a proper upbringing—"an idyllic childhood," he says—for tuning him in to the needs and strengths of others, and for helping him develop the deep, "innate" sense of discipline that drives him to such great heights. (His accomplishments include being named one of *Time Magazine's* 100 Most Influential People in the World in 2006 and one of ESPN's top ten point guards of all time.) Plus, Nash laughs just a few hours before game time, "I have a hard time sitting still," he says. A powerful balance of dreamer and pragmatist, a child who plainly told his mother that he would one day be a big star in the NBA and then tirelessly worked his way to the top without being the tallest or the strongest or the fastest guy in the gym, Nash considers his life to be blessed, and feels it's always a privilege to share those blessings with others—whether they need the assist or not . . . and who doesn't, really?

DECLARATION OF INDEPENDENCE. When I was in eighth grade, I told my mom I'd one day play for the NBA. It could very easily have not happened, in which case it would be a naïve statement. But a lot of greatness is born in naïveté. Sports came to me relatively quickly and easily, and I felt like, with practice, I could get better and better and better, and if I kept getting better and better and better then one day I could play professionally in the NBA. I really just had this feeling that good things were going to happen. I felt I could do it. On the other hand, I knew I'd have to work hard, and that's never been a problem for me.

WARRIOR ONE. My greatest gift is my discipline and my drive, more than any one thing I can do with the ball. Those qualities have always been there in me, innately. I've always been up for a challenge. I've never been happy without having a clear goal, something to fight for. It's the way I'm wired. It goes well with sports.

HAVING A BALL. Sharing the ball just makes sense to me, whether I'm playing soccer or hockey or basketball. These are *team* sports. It's more creative to set up your teammates. It's more fun, too. If you don't want to play with a team, there are other sports to pursue. I love being a part of a team. These are games and they should be fun, and for a team to have as much fun as it can, they need to share. Sharing the ball brings lots of pleasure to me. It's how the game was meant to be played.

DREAMING IN METAPHOR. In so many ways, life and sport are the same. It's about a state of mind, wanting to make the right decision, liking who you are, trying to grow and win from every opportunity, facing adversity, working as a team.

COMMUNICATION. Communication is paramount on the court, just as it is in life. The vast majority of that communication is nonverbal. You've got to be clear. You've got to be honest. You've got to be sensitive. And you've got to be paying attention. If you're genuine and motivated from a right place, you'll be effective in sports or in life.

HIGH POINTS. I've accomplished a lot in my career, but the high point isn't any one thing or any great moment. The high points happen periodically, and it's when my team is playing well, when my teammates and I are enjoying each other, when there's a sense that everything we're doing is communal, that everyone's heart and motives are in the right place. Those are the high points, when we're all in this together, striving to do and be more together.

FILM. From Kurosawa to Bergman, Woody Allen to Paul Thomas Anderson, I love it all. It's amazing the different ways that people speak the language of cinema and tell their stories and share their visions. It's a beautiful medium and language, and it's one I'll be working in more and more.

ALWAYS WANTING MORE. It's important to be in the moment, absolutely, enjoying the great connectivity we can have as a team. I'm also always a little bit on edge about what else I can do to be better, so that I'm not resting on my laurels. You have to always work hard and try hard to be more than you are.

THE LOVE THAT YOU GIVE. I had an incredible childhood, and a lot of kids don't. I got to travel the world, and I see how fortunate I was. There are a lot of inequalities in the world, things my parents pointed out to me as a child, which I'm even more aware of today. You have to see this in the world. You have to understand it. It feels compelling to me —*natural*— to get involved in helping improve the lives of others. It's important, and it's really fun. It's a mission, not just the moments.

WHERE THE HEART IS. My parents, my wife, my kids, my friends, they're the bedrock, the foundation. I can't imagine life without them, and I can't imagine enjoying any of the other blessings in my life without them. They make my life worth living.

Joyce Carol Oates
on gratitude

*"My sense of reality has been
conditioned by
(Alice in Wonderland), certainly,
and I am grateful for it."*

HERE'S THE PROBLEM WITH BEING PROLIFIC, with writing, say, two books a year for the past four decades, not to mention countless short stories, plays, essays, poems, and pieces of cultural criticism. The problem is this: At some point, through the sheer law of averages, you're bound to be terrible. Unless you are Joyce Carol Oates, that is. Born in 1938, raised in a working-class farming town in upstate New York, schooled in the same one-room building as her mother, Oates is today known as the "Dark Lady of American Letters," owing to the shadowy characters and themes that slink and explode through her work. She is one of literature's most prolific writers, which frequently confounds readers and critics alike. In 2007, literary critic Michael Dirda wondered, "How does one judge a new book by Joyce Carol Oates when one is not familiar with most of the backlist? Where does one start?" The answer: *anywhere*. One National

Book Award (for 1968's *them*) and three Pulitzer Prize nominations (for *Black Water*, *What I Lived For*, and *Blonde*) do not lie. Oates, who has been a professor of creative writing at Princeton since 1978, began writing at fourteen, pounding out stories on a manual typewriter gifted to her by an eccentric grandmother. Her voracious readings of William Faulkner, the Brontë sisters, and Dostoyevsky undoubtedly influenced her creative concerns, which include issues of sexuality, class tensions, power struggles, and physical and spiritual pugilism. Oates's narratives frequently read like remembered dreams that spring shockingly, violently, lucidly to life, oftentimes with the smallest detail. The stories are humid, cast in shadows, taut. Blood makes noise in an Oates story, and the bodies are always warm—whether the author is approaching boxers or pedophiles, demons or matinee idols, Bob Dylan or bigots. Like her favorite literary hero, Alice, Oates long ago went through the looking glass, and her reports from the other side are as vivid, brilliant, and essential as they are numerous, gifts for which every reader should be most grateful.

CARROLL OF THE BELLE. I was only about eight years old when I first read Lewis Carroll's *Alice in Wonderland*, and when we're very, very young almost anything that comes into our lives that's special or unique or profound can have the effect of changing us. I didn't read other books that I might have at that age, like *The Wind in the Willows*. It's one of those strange things. The *Alice in Wonderland* books that came to me at that age really made a profound impact upon on me. I virtually memorized most of *Alice*. When I began writing as a little girl, with crayons, I emulated the idea of that book—it had to be a book with a cover and illustrations and a title page and a spine with a name on it. It was sort of like an artifact I was creating, a wonderful, three-dimensional, intellectual toy of some kind. That blend of the surreal and the nightmare of the quotidian have always stayed with me. My sense of reality has been conditioned by that book, certainly, and I am grateful for it.

LIGHTING THE FUSE. I love to read. Reading, especially good books, makes me excited and kind of restless, and I feel like I want to write, too. It may have nothing to do with being influenced directly by what I've read, but it ignites the creativity in me. Say you have a musical inclination and you hear somebody playing wonderful jazz piano. You immediately want to run out and do something like that, even if you weren't necessarily *influenced*. It's somehow an awakening or a quickening of interest and excitement. I write, basically, so that I can read sometime in the future a text that didn't exist before, and with the hope that it will somehow amaze me.

CAMPFIRES AND CAVE WALLS. The impulse to tell stories—to present a certain point of view or perspective—is part of our species. There is a storytelling instinct in everyone. Sometimes it comes out in very formalized ways, where the person is actually a writer and works in the context of traditional forms, or the person is an oral storyteller. Many of us know people, are related to people, who cannot write anything at all, an uncle or a grandfather, but who can, nevertheless, tell wild and amusing stories. This is an instinct that goes across all boundaries. When you come to the so-called artist, that's a person who has this instinct, but looks to tradition and sees how this instinct has been accommodated in the past. Artists look to predecessors, so it's more formalized and intellectualized. I don't consider it unnatural. Politicians are storytellers. The word today in politics and media is "spinning"; that's part of the storytelling tradition. It's part of our instinct as human beings.

THIS WOMAN'S WORK. People have no idea how much I revise. It's always thought that I write very quickly. If anyone could see how much revision I do, people would shake their heads, and say, "Why would she work so hard?" My threshold of misery and frustration, it must be very high, because I do things that require a work ethic, and a level of misery, that is rare for anyone to undertake electively. To whip something off very quickly and send it out would have no pleasure for me at all. I would never do that. I labor over everything.

A HARD DAY'S NIGHT. Each book is like building up from the ground. You're laying a foundation, fumbling for the materials you need; you're building, it falls down, a wind comes along, a flood, and your building slowly and laboriously and arduously comes along. Once the structure's done, you give it away or sell it. Most writers are working at way below the minimum wage, if you figure out how much we make an hour. With me, it's like forty-nine cents, I'm sure. But it's my *life*, you know.

Dolly Parton
on gratitude

"I was born with a happy heart. I wake up every day expecting things to be right, and if they're not I get to making them right."

IT'S BEEN SAID A MILLION TIMES: Good things come in small packages. The maxim may as well have been coined for country-western music legend Dolly Parton who is barely tall enough to ride amusement park roller coasters even today. Raised six decades ago with eleven siblings in a one-room cabin in a small town of less than 1,000 people, Parton is nevertheless, a pop-culture Gulliver, an icon a thousand times larger and exponentially more significant than her humble, diminutive roots would suggest. It's hard to resist casting *The Dolly Parton Story* as a modern-day fairy tale. Parton—who claims an over-sized satchel of nicknames, including Smokey Mountain Song-bird, Iron Butterfly, Queen of Country, Backwoods Barbie, and Queen of Nashville—may have been born small and dirt poor, but by today's numbers she's as big as they come: twenty-five number one singles, forty-one top ten country albums, and a massively successful multimedia corporation (Dolly Parton Enterprises) worth nine figures. In making it big, Parton didn't stop at leaving her mark on music; we also know and love her for her vast collection of platinum wigs, not to mention that almost cartoonishly glorious hour-glass figure — "all bought and paid for," Parton is quick to crack. When it comes right down to it, regardless of size, spark, or origins, Parton knows exactly what she's doing, and executes it all with a good spirit, a grateful heart, and an "I think I can" perseverance. "There's a heart beneath the boobs and a brain beneath the wigs," Parton once famously said — which is why she was singing on regional television at the age of twelve, recording bubble-gum singles in Nashville at thirteen, becoming a minor sensation and honing her chops with country music Svengali Porter Wagoner on national TV, before becoming a superstar in her own right in the 1970s and 1980s. Grammys, box-office hits, television smashes, and cultural lioness status were all showered upon Dolly, as she rose to stardom, following work that included "Here You Come Again," "You're the Only One," "Islands in the Stream" (with Kenny Rogers), and the still ubiquitous "I Will Always Love You," not to mention the films *9 to 5*, *The Best Little Whorehouse in Texas*, and *Steel Magnolias*. That Parton's life has been blessed is inarguable, and she knows it with a smile, which is why today, still recording music as actively as ever — and married to Carl Dean, a man she met in a Nashville Laundromat forty-four years ago — Parton also devotes a tremendous amount of time to giving back — oftentimes to children, those other "good things in small packages." (Her Imagination Library promotes literacy and reading in children under five, worldwide.) Eventually, Parton's life and work seem to say, we all make it big.

THE FAMILY THAT SINGS TOGETHER. I was totally blessed with a musical family. Some of my earliest and greatest influences were in my own family and that was a great blessing. We were always singing and playing and writing. There was always music. Today, a lot of my family actually works with me. I've always said, if I have a dime, they have a nickel.

THE ROAD TO COMPASSION. I think being brought up dirt poor left me with a feeling of what it was like to go without, so I can relate when people are having a hard time. In my case, being a songwriter, I'm able to write not only for and about myself, but for what I know other people are feeling, even if they don't always have the means to get their voices heard.

SNAPPING OUT OF THE SADNESS. We're meant to be happy, but we have to work at that. I was born with a happy heart. I wake up every day expecting things to be right, and if they're not, I get to making them right. It's very important that people have a good attitude, which is what my song, "Better Get to Livin'" is about. Sometimes people like to wallow in their sorrows and their sad tales, but I really believe that's detrimental to the lives we should be living. It's natural to have hurts and disappointments, but you have to deal with it—pray out of it, dream out of it, and get to living.

FIRST TIME'S THE CHARM. I was maybe thirteen years old, and I had recorded some songs, including "Puppy Love," which I had written, but nothing much had happened yet career-wise. One day, I was at home, sitting up on the sink, cleaning out some cabinets. The radio was playing and then my song came on. I jumped off the counter and slipped all over the floor, because somebody had been mopping it, and I turned up that radio. I'll never, ever forget hearing my voice coming out of that little box that I had heard so many great voices come out of. There I was on the radio. I thought, "This is gonna be good. I'm gonna like this!"

THE GUIDING LIGHT. Porter Wagoner gave me my first really big break. He was a friend and a mentor and a collaborator. It wasn't until Porter took me on his show (the syndicated *Porter Wagoner Show*, which broadcast nearly 700 episodes in twenty-one years on the air) so many years ago as his featured female singer that I got exposed to the broader public. That really opened up my career. It was from that that all the other great things in my life have happened. My name will always be paired somewhere with Porter's, and I will always be proud of that.

When Porter died (in 2007), it was like a piece of me died, too, but I also know that a piece of Porter will always live in the music I make.

THE BOOK LADY. A lot of years ago, I started the Imagination Library to put books in the hands of children, one a month, from the day they're born until they're in kindergarten. We started in my home county and today we're in forty-seven states, 700 counties, and we're starting up in Canada and England. It's really a wonderful way to get books to children, when they're most impressionable and ready to learn. My own father was not able to read and write, and that's true of so many mountain people, even today; they have to work so hard to make ends meet that they don't get the education they need. My father was so proud of this program. He loved it when kids would call me the "Book Lady."

LOVE THIS LIFE. I've been writing since I was seven years old. I write something all the time. Never a week goes by—never a day—when I'm not writing. Inspiration comes from everything. I'm touched by life. I'm touched by love. I've got a keen ear and a sharp wit, and I just can't help myself. I truly have a love in my heart for people and a love in my heart for life.

THE LOVE THAT YOU TAKE. Everything I do, all of these blessings, everything I give, it all comes back to me ten-fold. I just give it away, everything I can, everything about me. It's always a cycle. I give. It comes back to me. Then I energize it and put it right back out there. That's just the way I share, and it's the best blessing of all to me.

Zachary Quinto
on gratitude

"I'm grateful someone showed me how to be disciplined and respectful in this profession."

BEFORE THE DOOR is an undergraduate acting exercise in which performers play out their preparations for turning the knob of an imaginary door, behind which an intense situation awaits them. As metaphors go, Before the Door may aptly summarize the life and times of Zachary Quinto. Today, best known for his eerily sedate, brain-chomping über-villain Sylar on NBC's *Heroes* and his deeply Zen turn as Spock in the recent *Star Trek* reboot, Quinto, born in 1977, stood before the door for decades until landing his star-making gigs, and sees a metropolis of doorways still ahead, images of infinite possibility and choice. (Immediately ahead: a *Star Trek* sequel and an opportunity to play George Gershwin in Steven Spielberg's recently announced biopic.) Born and raised in Pittsburgh, a seven-year-old Quinto found comfort, release, and a second home in the local theater scene, a welcome distraction from his father's untimely passing. Grief looks very different when one is playing a Munchkin who mellifluously treads the yellow brick road. An axle-busting car accident in his teen years codified Quinto's commitment to the theater arts and he enrolled in Carnegie Mellon's renowned drama program, working consciously for the first time with the imaginary door, an exercise that so captured his imagination he would later dub his own multimedia company, Before the Door Productions. Quinto was given clear passage to Los Angeles, almost immediately landing his first on-camera gig, hawking a hyper-caffeinated citrus soda, followed by a sudden, if uncommon, surge of guest spots on television. However, if fame is a fickle friend, as it has been posited, then so is steady work for up-and-coming thespians, and Quinto grew frustrated by the sporadic offers of work on mediocre programs, not to mention the thankless shifts, shilling pate, and Arnold Palmers at Los Angeles eateries. "I felt, as many actors do, that I was meant to do more than I was given the opportunity to do," he told *Carnegie Mellon Today* in 2007. And then a series of doors flew open in rapid succession: a season-long stint on *24*, a memorable turn on Tori Spelling's kitschy *So NoTORIous*, the work on *Heroes*, and the chance to play one of science fiction's greatest icons, Mr. Spock. By remaining open, grateful, and always prepared—this is an actor who learned to give the Vulcan salute by rubber banding his fingers together day and night, after all—Quinto has determined that the best way to approach a door is by being the key.

CITY OF CHAMPIONS. Pittsburgh was such a supportive community, the place I grew up, and so beautiful, too. It's a very solid performing arts town with a great theater scene. That theater scene is very well extended to the children in the community. It's where I got my start. So many kids that I used to perform with back then are making their livelihoods from performing today, and that's an amazing thing. Without Pittsburgh, I don't know that I'd have what I have today, by way of confidence or experience or accomplishments.

HOUSEKEEPING IN OZ. I was in a production of *The Wizard of Oz* when I was a kid. It was my first show. I was playing a Munchkin, like all the kids were. The first dress rehearsal, I left the theater and went home. My costume, which I had just left on the floor of the dressing room, was folded up the next day, very neatly, with a note attached to it from our costume lady, this very formidable, stern woman with a heavy European accent: "You always hang up your costume." I never forgot that. It's probably done me good in this career. I'm grateful someone showed me how to be disciplined and respectful in this profession.

HOLDING OUT FOR A HERO. Growing up, I was told all the time by professors and guest speakers and mentors, *if you can imagine yourself doing something other than acting, then do it*. I never took it seriously until I was an out-of-work actor for a long time, and then I realized: There is nothing else I can imagine doing. I'm grateful I never walked away from acting, which I *did* consider many times—right before I got *Heroes*.

SOUNDTRACK OF OUR LIVES. I've always underscored my life with great music. I can't imagine life without it. It's always been a huge part of my creative process, though it was a lot harder to use my iPod with those Vulcan ears on. *(laughs)* I don't know if Spock has a theme song, or not. It would probably be Leonard Nimoy's version of "The Ballad of Bilbo Baggins." But that's Leonard's territory. I don't think I'll be cutting a remake anytime soon.

BLOOD BROTHERS. My closest friends are all of my classmates from college, and we completely sustain each other. They didn't care when I was unemployed, and they don't care that I am doing well today, and it's important—especially in this industry—to be surrounded by those kinds of people. I'll always be the same guy to them, whatever the circumstances might be.

TAKING REALITY BY SURPRISE. I chuckle in joy whenever I think about the word "surprise," especially as it applies to my life. Surprise is a word I try to live by. I invite it all the time into my experience, into the roles I play. It keeps you present. It keeps you alive. It keeps you interesting.

LIVING LONG AND PROSPERING. I wasn't ready to cut my Spock hair for a long time after we finished shooting the movie, though I was grateful when my eyebrows grew back. (*laughs*) It's a role that does change you and, for me, I can't say how amazing it was to have Leonard Nimoy (the original Spock) always there, offering his intimate guidance. Whatever people take from my Spock in these movies, they need to know: It's all because Leonard was there for me.

BEFORE THE DOOR. I'm really learning in my life to understand that every gift or opportunity sprouts from a challenge or a conflict. We live in a chaotic time. We live chaotic lives. I can appreciate the light and the dark today, and wouldn't have the things in my life that I do without those challenges. It's just a matter of perspective.

Anne Rice
on gratitude

"In moving into our own house, we were able to surround ourselves with beauty . . . that meant everything at the time."

FOR THREE DECADES, Anne Rice wandered through darkness, looking for the light, just as her characters did—the nefariously soulful bloodsuckers of Rice's much-adored series, *The Vampire Chronicles*. Born Howard Allen O'Brien (after her father) in 1941, Rice was raised in the Catholic schools of New Orleans and Texas, then trekked through Hippie-era Haight-Ashbury with her childhood sweetheart, artist and writer Stan Rice, always in search of a place to belong. When the young couple's daughter Michele succumbed to leukemia at the age of five, Rice unwittingly transmuted her paralyzing grief into *Interview with the Vampire*, the novel that would launch a ten-book franchise and a movie most of us will never forget. Rice's bloodsuckers, widely credited with launching the vampire craze of this century, were royalty and vagabonds, pretenders and tricksters, hollowed from centuries of yearning, gone adrift for all that they miss or have never known. Simply put, they were outcasts long-ing to belong. Not unlike their creator. "I figured that was all of us," she says, matter-of-factly. After losing her husband of forty-one years, Rice abandoned Louisiana to be closer to her son, Christopher, in California. Having returned to Catholicism, she has spent the past decade penning religious-themed novels, including a reverent trilogy about the life of Jesus Christ, as well as a potent autobiography, *Called Out of Darkness: A Spiritual Confession.* If, as Leonard Cohen says, our broken places are where the light is most able to shine through, then Rice has offered her fractures to the world with grace and gratitude.

A FIFTH GRADE NOTHING. I sat down and wrote a book in the fifth grade. Of course, it wasn't *really* a novel. To me, as a child, it cer-tainly was. I wrote it in what, at the time, was called a twenty-five-cent notebook, which really is a quite thick notebook. I wrote on both sides of the pages and even drew a few little illustrations here and there. It was a science fiction story about a brother and sister who lived on Mars and came to Earth and picked up a man named Jimmy and told him all about Mars. In the end, they turn their spaceship around and heroically drive themselves straight into the sun. The reason this was heroic—and this is the big twist ending—is that they could not return to Mars because that planet's great disgrace was it still had slavery—that was my big surprise ending. Rather than return to a state of slavery on Mars, they drove their spaceship into the sun. What was so great about the experience is that all my friends liked the book so much. The oldest sister of a friend said that it was like actually reading a real, published book. That was just wonder-ful. I'm sure it's what set me to being a writer.

CLACKETY-CLACK. My stepmother, who was a very practical, wonderful woman, took me into Dallas before I went into college to buy me a typewriter. We went into these junk shops, really, the used stores, and she tested all of them. I remember she rejected a lot of them because they simply weren't fast enough. At the time, I didn't think too much about it, but she really did do me a service there. She picked out this wonderful little portable one, black and white keys, and it was real fast. I still have it. I won't give it up.

SLOW READING. One of the reasons I am a slow reader is that I hear every word out loud. I hook in best with fiction in which there is a musical quality, because I am hearing it. Hearing the music requires slow reading. When I was younger, I fell in love with Charles Dickens and with the novel *Great Expectations*. Almost every sentence in that book is beautifully written. The rhythm of the paragraphs to me was something I could really grab onto, but I read it at a snail's pace because I was hearing it. I never could compete with my friends who learned very early on to simply read, not hear. Often times, when I'm writing, I am actually talking out loud. People will come into the room and say I look like a madwoman, because there I am mumbling all the words and making all the faces. I'm not mad. I'm not possessed. I'm just hearing it. I'm speaking the book as I write it.

LOSS AND REBIRTH. It was after (my daughter's) death that I wrote *Interview with the Vampire*. I didn't, at the time, consciously think that the child vampire Claudia had anything to do with my daughter. I was simply wound up in the story and figuring out what it was really like to be a vampire. In reflection, of course, I see the whole thing as being allegorical—it was about grief for my lost faith and, certainly, grief for my lost daughter. Claudia was a little girl who never grew up, who met a horribly violent end, and she was, obviously, inspired by my daughter's death. I just didn't see it at the time.

HITTING THE LIST. It was life-changing (becoming a bestselling author). We could, for the first time, do things like buy a house and travel to Europe. Those are the first two enormously important things we did. In moving into our own house, we were able to surround ourselves with beauty. Out every window we could see beautiful things. And then, just wandering around Europe was wonderful. I took two trips there in two years, and that had really been a lifelong dream. There had never before been a possibility for any of that. There simply wasn't any money.

Suddenly, we were able to. That was absolutely fantastic. That meant everything at the time. The world opened up in those hours.

THE BIG EASY. I am missing it right now, and it's agony. I wake up in the morning missing it. I wake up often in shock and disbelief that I'm not in my house there in the Garden District. (The city is) so laid-back, but it has so much energy. There are people there, of all kinds, who are so creatively involved in life, and yet they are not in the American rat race. It's a very strange kind of energy, and it affects everybody. I think the city was much misjudged in this regard after Katrina. A lot of the people we assumed were the poor and forgotten people of New Orleans, based on what we saw on the television, weren't that at all. These people may have more or less things than you or I, but they're richer for sure because they love the place they are.

THE LOVE THAT YOU MAKE. I was not a writer who ever got any energy from writing about characters I hated, which is uncommon in America. There are many writers who build entire careers writing about people they scorn and despise and want to eviscerate. I'm not that kind of writer. I write about characters I love, and people responded to that, I believe.

Seth Rogen
on gratitude

> " . . . They say I'm being low-key
> about it all. They say I'm non-
> plused. What does it mean to be
> plused? If it would make me seem
> more appreciative, I'll be plused."

SURELY, THE GERMANS had Seth Rogen in mind when they coined the phrase "wunderkind." By twenty-six Rogen had become the voice of his generation, a comedic everyman-child, lovable despite his onscreen propensity for weed and crotch-centric bon mots and an utter ineffectuality in the bedroom, boardroom, and battlefield. Truth told, Rogen has been killing since Hebrew school. In his teen years, he was crowned the second-funniest person in Canada. In the Zeitgeist-capturing, machine gun salvo of *Knocked Up*, *Superbad*, and *Pineapple Express*, Rogen became, gulp, the new American male, Peter Pan as pot-head, Iron John as slacker, Cary Grant by way of Beavis and Butthead. This is an intensely frightening prospect if you're looking to lay railroad track through South Dakota or mine coal from the earth's soulless core, but a deeply heartening notion if, like so many twentysomething dudes, your biggest problems are how to shave your own back or clear cookies from your browser. Check Rogen's box office track record if you need further evidence that he is, if only barely arguably, fast leaving a cultural imprint on the new millennium. Rogen's been tickling funny bones for most of his life, the offspring of liberal Canadians who actually loved him a lot, a schoolyard hero for his quick wit and raunchy patois, a national celebrity by puberty, thanks to his successful stand-up work. When Rogen moved to Los Angeles in the late '90s, he already had his first pro gig lined up, costarring in *Freaks and Geeks*, created by mentor Judd Apatow. Though the show, and its Apatow-helmed encore, *Undeclared*, was quickly canceled, it led to bigger and better things (an Emmy-nominated stint writing for *Da Ali G Show*, lumbering, rapier-witted sidekick roles in *Anchorman* and *The 40-Year-Old Virgin*). Today, Rogen is a bona fide movie star and a booming movie mogul, a writer, director, producer, an *auteur*—if such a phrase can be applied to a moviemaker whose onscreen characters discuss male cameltoe and facial circumcision—already afforded, even at his tender age, tremendous respect. Rogen, who punctuates every other sentence with a gruff, endearing giggle, takes none of this for granted, but is loving every minute of it.

THE UNBEARABLE LIGHTNESS OF BEING "SWEET." I've had a lot of men call me sweet lately. I'm having extensive conversations about my sweetness. (*laughs*) I'm getting used to it. I'm coming to terms with it. The truth is, I *am* sweet. I've never been a jerky guy. I've never been mean to chicks or been an asshole to my friends. I'm the guy who's at home writing jokes and reading comic books. I think people who really know me would be surprised if I was suddenly Hollywood's new bad boy.

HEAD ON STRAIGHT, EH? I'm from Canada, and I partied a lot in high school. In Canada, you can drink alcohol a few years younger than kids in America can, so maybe we just get it out of our system earlier. I'm all good now. *That's* good.

REAL GENIUS. I'm like New Coke compared to someone like Sacha Baron Cohen, whom I had the privilege of working for. I think he's absolutely a genius. I think he's doing something I'm not doing, innovation-wise, originality-wise, and even humor-wise in many ways. Maybe it's because I'm just acting in straight-out movies, which is nice and relatable. But I, personally, think Sacha is the voice of a new comedic generation. He's brilliant.

CHILD'S PLAY. I love the fact that I get to have fun for work every day. I'm very psyched about everything that's going on in my life. I don't know how people think I should respond, but they say I'm being low-key about it all. They say I'm nonplused. What does it mean to be plused? If it would make me seem more appreciative, I'll be plused. Just tell me how. Honestly, I'm as happy as I can be.

ACTING ONE'S AGE. I've always felt older than I am, and a lot of the people I work with tend to feel younger than they are. That's a phenomenon I find interesting. I work with a lot of people who are much older than me who act much more immaturely than I do. (*laughs*) Some people don't grow up. I don't know if that's an old thing or a new thing. Peter Pan's been around for a long time. *Finding Neverland* taught me that. (*laughs*) People have not wanted to grow up since they started growing up in the first place.

GOOD GENES. As far back as I can remember, funny is in my family. My parents are hilarious. My grandparents are hilarious. Everybody in my life is funny. My family is very loud and very laughing. I'm grateful for that.

THE EARLY JOKES. My early stand-up comedy was all about grandparents and hand jobs. Those were my two major categories. I killed, man. When I was sixteen, I was called the second-funniest guy in Canada. Canada being the second-largest country in the world, I might actually have been the second-funniest guy in the entire world. (*laughs*)

WHAT FUNNY IS. I think everything's funny, honestly. I think there's humor everywhere. I'm the guy that hears a movie idea, and it's a drama, and I laugh because I think it's hilarious. I laugh at everything. Comedy is everywhere—it's in the dick jokes *and* it's in the funeral. It all makes me laugh. My job is to convey what I think is funny to people who may not see the world the way I do.

Maya Rudolph
on gratitude

"I think of (my mom) often when I'm parenting my own children, and it always makes me laugh. I wonder if she was amazed as often as I am that these children actually listen and follow directions. (laughs) . . . I do live for these girls."

MOST OF US HAVE NEVER HAD a lullaby penned in our honor, let alone by our mother and father. Rarer still is a custom lullaby, "Lovin' You," crooned in a definitive, spellbinding rendition by Mom, that goes on to become a pop-music staple, a latter-day romantic standard, ubiquitous at weddings and on radio dedication shows. Then, for good measure, that's your actual given name cascading through the song's dynamic, octave-pirouetting outro in your mother's falsetto. You're three at the time. By the time you're seven, your mother will fall to breast cancer. Thirty years later, you'll be a beloved and respected comedienne voicing a fairy-tale character in *Shrek*, a billion-dollar motion picture franchise, in which that lullaby—*your* very own, personal bedtime song—serves as a riotous joke, its scale-clambering climax causing a quaintly animated bluebird to explode into a grisly pond of feathers and dust. This is the sweet, sour, unexpected, and irreverent life story of Maya Rudolph; that is, minus the two-year stint she enjoyed touring the world with alternative rock band the Rentals or falling in love with Paul Thomas Anderson, one of today's most respected filmmakers, or becoming a break-out star on *Saturday Night Live*, or giving birth to two lovely daughters of her own, or establishing herself as a leading actress of extraordinary depth and vulnerability in films like 2009's *Away We Go*. Indeed, a summary of Rudolph's life only suggests, and barely, that it has been almost supernaturally charmed, even when the levy of heartache occasionally breaks, as with the untimely passing of her mother, Minnie Riperton. At the center of this life story is Rudolph herself, beautiful and a bona fide chameleon all at once, possessed of an uncanny, Zeligesque proclivity for vanishing into the scenery until the perfect moment presents itself to spark intelligent, absurdist chaos. Rudolph, born in 1972, is a mistress of disguise, capable of playing any ethnicity, a nimble acrobat with accents, addicted quite possibly to wigs, wielding a comic scalpel (not hand grenades) on her targets. Who else could play Oprah Winfrey and Paris Hilton, Tyra Banks and Liza Minnelli, and be equally convincing as *all* of them? With Rudolph, it's "now you see her, now you don't," but even when you're *seeing* her, are you really seeing *her* at all? Rudolph is a mischief-maker lying in wait, an inspired and inspiring heroine of a thousand faces. In saying grace, reflecting on her life's many blessings, the real Rudolph emerges from the woodwork, from the blur of make-believe and comic invention. The woman we're seeing, and we are really seeing her in this hour of gratitude, is innocent, playful, vulnerable, and perfectly lovely—the kind of girl for whom lullabies were undoubtedly invented and wars were once waged.

AMNESIA. *Saturday Night Live* is like childbirth. Whenever I try to remember it, I go completely blank. I don't even remember half the things that went on the air, or the things that might have been cut. But I do remember it was a pretty good time, and I felt a lot of love. There was a spark beneath every live show. I'm grateful for that.

WHEN YOU'RE A JET. When you've got good partners, a great gang, you can do anything because you know you'll never fall on your face. And if you do fall on your face somehow, that gang will be around to laugh at you. And then, hopefully, they'll pick you up. Or maybe they won't. But it's very freeing knowing you can fall. I'm grateful to have had that.

ROSEANNE ROSEANNADANNA. Gilda Radner was insanely funny, but when I was a kid I also felt deeply connected with whatever she was doing on TV. She was so sweet and so human. That humanity always came through in her work. I never knew her, and I don't think I wanted to be her, but I did want to be her best friend. It got complicated, though, because I was also madly in love with Gene Wilder. I could not wait to marry Gene Wilder. So sickly funny. Such amazing eyes. Turns out, they were married.

THIS MAMA SAYS. I would be a Grinch if I didn't believe parenthood was the most moving thing in the world. I don't have a hard heart like that. I do cherish every moment I have where I am entrusted with these little creatures, and have to fill them with a sense of the world and right and wrong and everything else. Of course, the oldest is five now, so she's almost done with me.

WIGS. On *Saturday Night Live*, it was always a lucky thing, I thought, to be able to play anybody I wanted because of the way I look. I never thought, "Oh, if I put on this wig, I can cross racial boundaries and be white or Asian or Latina." I'm not a barrier-cracker. I'm no Norma Rae. But I do love wigs, and I do hate my real hair, and maybe it's all worked out well. I don't think I'd wear wigs around the house. I don't think it would be sexy to be with my man and have my wig fall off. That's kind of a bummer.

LOVIN' YOU. I hope I have the goodness in me that my mom did. She was a very special human being. I think of her often when I'm parenting my own children, and it always makes me laugh. I wonder if she was amazed as often as I am that these children actually listen and follow directions. (*laughs*) Living for another person is a completely different universe, and I *do* live for these girls. It was interesting giving birth and then going back to *SNL*. I was the only mom there. Everybody on the show would do their extended college thing—do your work, go out to party until 4 A.M., and I would make my way home to hold my baby, happy about it.

THE ALOHA STATE OF MIND. I'm very grateful that Hawaii exists. I thank Hawaii every time I'm there. I really wish Hawaii would allow me to live there. I am a whining, screaming kid every time I have to leave.

GREEN ACRES. As fat as they make you, I am really grateful for avocados. I grew up in California where you could always get a great avocado. When I first went to New York, I was so surprised; avocados are not so easy to get there, and I thought, "What kind of place is this anyway?"

BASKIN-ROBBINS MINT AND CHIP ICE CREAM. Also very green. Also one of my favorite things in the world.

I WRITE THE SONGS. Music means the world to me, and I always think I'm going to make some great, funky album, but I'm still here on my butt acting and doing comedy and being a parent and talking to you. I *do* love writing parody songs. Doing that is easy as breathing for me. But a real album? We'll see. Maybe I should go do that right now. You know what? I'll call you back in an hour.

Liev Schreiber
on gratitude

"I'm blessed to have discovered the theater. It gave me somewhere to belong."

WE KNOW HIM TODAY BECAUSE OF A MAGICAL ASS many yesterdays ago. To be fair, it was a Shakespearean ass. A donkey to be clear. Bottom in *A Midsummer Night's Dream*, to be exact. As bass clarinetist in his junior high school's orchestra, young Liev Schreiber—named for Tolstoy, with a surname meaning "writer" in German—bore witness to the visceral, instantaneous reception audiences afforded the playful beast's double entendre and elegant chicanery and decided, then and there, the actor's life was for him. Some three decades later and Schreiber is among our very finest actors, leavening his formidable figure and booming voice with a vulnerability, humanity, and quiet sadness in films like *Scream*, *The Manchurian Candidate*, *RKO 281*, *Wolverine*, and *The Painted Veil*. Born in 1967, Schreiber enjoyed a vagabond childhood, moving frequently, a perennial outsider, following his hippie mother from one adventure to the next, soaking up all of the classic cinema he could in the nation's repertory theaters. Charlie Chaplin was an early favorite—no surprise to audiences familiar with Schreiber's intensely agile performances. Trained formally at Yale University School of Drama and London's Royal Academy of Dramatic Art, Schreiber has split his career fairly evenly between treading the boards in the world's most legendary theaters and gracing the silver screen in films of varying scope, ambition, and genre. In all of his work, he is superb. Still, Schreiber is no movie star, steadfastly avoiding the pitfalls of celebrity, and he'd have it no other way. Instead, Schreiber, a devout New Yorker and father of two with actress Naomi Watts, is an actor and an artist, an individual who celebrates his good fortune, even as he questions its value to the rest of the world. It's a life of quiet gratitude that Schreiber lives, the drama left to bards and their talking mules, or the fools in Tinseltown.

FOOTLIGHTS CALLING. At a very young age, I knew that I wasn't very good at the things you have to be good at to be successful in the world: composure, mathematics, social stuff. Everything you need for success, I thought, were all the things I was awful at. But I did know I had a feel for other things—music, literature, rhythm. I just had no idea how I would ever fit in, let alone succeed. I'm blessed to have discovered the theater. It gave me somewhere to belong.

CHILD'S PLAY. I have to admit, it feels like I never stopped playing. My life has just been a lark, one long series of goofs. But I take goofs very seriously.

INTERNATIONAL MAN OF MYSTERY. Actors need to retain a little bit of mystery. That is important. Audiences should not be looking at the actor when they go to the movies; they should be looking at the character. I believe in the power of transformation, so I'd prefer it if audiences weren't looking at me and thinking about my life or my exploits. I'd like them to look at the character and see themselves. It's my job, to a certain degree, to get people thinking about their own lives. Not mine.

MIXED NUTS. I'd like to believe that acting is easy. But when it comes to drag queens? No. All bets are off. It sucks. First of all, being shaved from head to toe, then those shoes, then the wigs—put a bowl of fire on my head and stick me in the head with eighteen pins. It's not easy being a lady.

KISS KISS BANG BANG. As much as I hate guns, if you put one in my hand, I can't help but want to do a somersault and hide behind a tree. Acting can be a lot of fun for a boy who never grew up.

DÉJÀ VU FOR YOU. That's honestly the joy of acting: Not only do you get to use your life experiences, but you get to feel them all over again, too.

DARWIN IN DIAPERS. I firmly believe that everyone's got a great story, whether or not they acknowledge it or a journalist acknowledges it. It's impossible to survive in this life and not have a good story. Just being alive is such a remarkable thing. I have kids now, and I watch them walk and I go, "Holy shit! How the hell did they do that?" I think it's remarkable that we make it to fifteen. Jesus, I made it to fifteen. That's amazing. They should make a movie out of that: I made it to fifteen. You get some perspective on that when you become a parent.

PAID TO PLAY. Between you and me, acting's not as difficult as some people make it out to be. When I really think about it, I can't get over my luck. The travel alone is pretty outstanding. I get to go to places like Eastern Europe, live in these great hotels, visit these countries, all expenses paid. It's a pretty cushy gig.

BEING THERE. Peter Sellers. Jerzy Kosinski. Hal Ashby. Perfection.

SECRET O' LIFE. It's about allowing yourself to make mistakes. It's about taking risks. It's about being ready to make a fool of yourself. You have to be ready to fail. You have to work with people who are tolerant of your risks and failures. That goes for whatever you're doing in life, I imagine.

Mike Shinoda

on gratitude

"Being successful wouldn't be worth it if I had to travel that path with people I didn't like."

THERE ARE NO OVERDOSES HERE, or decapitated Chiroptera, no headboards turned to sawdust for all the notching or annihilated plasmas that decorate the sidewalks below penthouse suites. The so-called "good old days" of rock 'n' roll are dead. *Viva la revolucion!* While metal rockers of yesteryear were egocentric demolition men, anarchists, outlaws, and lunatics, today's metal superstar is a different animal altogether, one more inclined to spark a genuine revolution than a nickel bag. No one personifies this twenty-first century rock 'n' roll superstar better than Mike Shinoda, cofounder, covocalist, rapper, keyboardist, and guru of the bestselling nu-metal unit Linkin Park. Shinoda, born in 1977, is a third-generation Japanese-American, born and raised in the hilly suburban sprawl of Agoura Hills, California, the kind of place where everyone's house looks the same, including the garages, one of which provided the womb and incubator for his multiplatinum band. Shinoda is married seven years to an author of children's books, remains close with his parents and siblings, and recounts a childhood that was downright idyllic. And yet there is a gale-force angst and aggression, though unerringly melodic, to the music he crafts with his Linkin Park bandmates. When the band rages, and it *does* rage, it's often not only on how the world *is*, but in how we've decided to perceive it for the past two decades. Shinoda does not suffer negativity or irony kindly, nor hypocrisy and self-delusion. "Life's too short," he says, nonplused. Perhaps the quantum shift in today's metal maestro reflects a spiritual or intellectual change in metal's primary consumers: the fans. Maybe all the blood-spitting and devil-worshipping that lasted from the Nixon age through the Reagan era was just shtick and showmanship. Today's music fan—illusions punctured by sour leadership, global war, economic collapse—demands earnestness, not irony, and above all, sincerity. Linkin Park provides the perfect gravity for their universe of fans, which Shinoda refers to as "a very connected culture." The band's message, if one wants to boil it down, is simple and Gandhi-esque: *Be the change you want to see in the world.* To that end, Shinoda lives a clean-cut, mindful, healthy lifestyle. He works hard on his relationships with his family and bandmates, though he probably toils even harder on making his band the best in the world—but the labor is never torturous. Shinoda is also a brilliant political and visual artist whose artwork, a poppy collision of digital and hand-drawn media, has been exhibited around the world. Closest to Shinoda's heart, and perhaps most representative of his belief that each human being is accountable to the next, is the nonprofit Linkin Park founded in 2005, Music For Relief (*www.musicforrelief.org*). The organization has raised more than $3 million, planted more than 800,000 trees, and sent aid in the aftermath of Hurricane Katrina, the tsunamis in South Asia, cyclones in Burma and Bangladesh, wildfires of California, and the devastating earthquake in Haiti. Clearly, Shinoda is a man of vision, and one that begins with his own bounty of gratitude.

KEYS TO THE KINGDOM. When I was five or six, my mother enrolled me in piano lessons, telling me, "It will look good on your college applications." I started with basic tunes, and eventually moved on to classical pieces, but reading from sheet music always bored or frustrated me. So I cheated. One day, after I played a new piece for my teacher, she said, "That sounded great, but next time I want you to actually *read* the sheet music." I asked how she knew I wasn't reading. She said, "Because you transposed the chords. You were playing by ear." I remember that her scolding was actually mixed with a little bit of pride: She knew I was getting good enough at playing—and had enough of an innate sense about music that I could play a piece from just hearing it. I've always seen that musical ability as a tremendous gift.

REBEL WITHOUT A PAUSE. I eventually started playing the stuff I was listening to: hip-hop. Once I found out that many of my favorite songs—by groups like A Tribe Called Quest and Public Enemy—were based on samples of jazz and blues records, that was it. I told my piano teacher I wanted to learn to play jazz, blues, and hip-hop. Lucky for me, she was smart enough to tell me she didn't know much about those things, and I should go elsewhere to learn more. I immediately bought a small keyboard and started building what ended up becoming a hip-hop production studio.

GIZMOS AND GADGETS. My phone is like a surplus memory bank for me: It stores all the stuff I want to remember, but can't. A program called Evernote keeps audio and text notes about work, blog ideas, restaurants, and gifts; iCal and Mac Mail keep my life organized. I'm online all day. I even found my dermatologist on yelp.com. Technology is a very good thing.

WHISTLE WHILE YOU WORK. I work hard, and I think it is a product of a few major contributors. Firstly: growing up, my mom and dad always had me do my homework before I was allowed to do anything else. Second: college. Art Center isn't like most schools; it was like having a 100-hour work week for three and a half years straight. Besides learning how to be a better artist, I built on some of the gifts I am most grateful for: craftsmanship, focus, cooperation, and humility.

RISING SON. My grandfather and grandmother had thirteen children, almost all here in the United States. They were both U.S. citizens when World War II began and had made a good business and good money. But they lived in California. When WWII broke out, the West Coast became an "exclusion zone." All Japanese—and many other Asians—who lived in California were removed from their homes and sent to internment camps for the duration of the war. When they got out, everything they had was destroyed or taken away. In 1988, my dad got a letter and a check from the U.S. government. The check was pretty substantial for us at the time, but the letter was more important. I read it over a few times with my dad, mom, and brother, and my parents told us how the government made a huge mistake in the '40s, and what a big deal this apology was. My parents wanted us to know that the internment showed us how the majority sometimes needs to speak up for the minority, especially when the minority can't speak up for themselves. My dad gave the money to our church, but kept the letter.

TRUE BLOOD: THE COURAGE OF CONVICTIONS. Yeah, we sold 14 million copies of our debut album, but we had to fight tooth and nail just to get that album recorded. It seemed like every step of the way was a new challenge that threatened to break the band up or distort our intentions with our music. We were told that we needed to make music more like this person or that; some said we needed a gimmick like other bands; I was even told I wasn't a good rapper, and that I should just play keyboards. Simply pushing through all that adversity and hearing the album finished—the way we wanted it, not anyone else's way—that was the real "gratitude moment."

BAND OF BROTHERS. A lot of people know that *Minutes to Midnight*, the album we released in 2007, was a departure for us musically. It didn't sound a lot like the albums we made before it, and it was a huge risk for us. But the story that a lot of people don't know was that, while we were breaking down our own creative barriers to make the album, we somehow managed to become better friends. Being successful wouldn't be worth it if I had to travel that path with people I didn't like. I'm so grateful for the guys in this band.

A JAPANESE HOMECOMING. This may seem strange, but when I got off the plane in Tokyo, I was greeted by a familiar sense that made a lot of the stress of playing there for the first time, go away. I recognized the smell of Japan, even though I had never been there before. The airport smelled like my aunt's house back in Los Angeles. I can't describe it, but it's a smell I recognize in most Japanese or Japanese-American homes, restaurants, or shops. I now joke with my family that some things "smell like Japan," and that usually brings to mind memories of eating huge plates of food at my aunt's house on New Year's Day. I'm grateful for that.

POSTER BOY. Shepard Fairey's story and his artwork resonate with me on all levels. He's a risk taker who knows the right balance between mainstream and subculture, success and credibility. He has a history on both sides of the law: He's been arrested for his graffiti and activism, but also created the iconic "Hope" image for Barack Obama that the whole world now knows. We need more artists like him.

EBB AND FLOW. I like the excitement of knowing that things are moving. I suppose I tend to have a pleasant feeling of dissatisfaction about my work. I like to find flaws in things and fix them, and I try to keep myself open to hearing criticism about places where I can improve. Movement is a blessing to me.

THE PERFECT DAY . . . is just the right balance of work and play, with my closest family and best friends.

Andrew Stanton

on gratitude

"I don't believe you can fake won-
der. You either sincerely arrive at it
or it entirely eludes you."

DEBATES WILL LIKELY RAGE ETERNAL over the greatest story ever told, but humbly submitted here and now is the
tale of Andrew Stanton. Twenty years ago, Stanton was just
another freshly scrubbed, nice guy with a knack for drawing, a
head full of dreams, and his adoring childhood sweetheart rooting unconditionally for his success. Even today, you may not
know Stanton by name. It's even less likely you know his face.
But by honoring the universal theme of "be true to yourself"
in both his personal life and his creative expression, Stanton,
born in 1965, has become one of the most critically and commercially successful filmmakers of all time, and quite possibly,
one of the happiest guys alive. Though the Boston-bred Stanton
had a stellar California Institute of the Arts pedigree and a stunning portfolio of animated work, Walt Disney Company failed
to hire him three times in the mid-'80s, which led him to seek

employment with an upstart animation company in Northern California. Stanton, who married the girl he fell in love with at fifteen, was the second animator, and the ninth employee overall, hired by Pixar. You see where this story is going. Working closely with Pixar founder, John Lasseter, Stanton channeled his inner child to cowrite a wildly imaginative, irreverent, deeply emotional tale of outcasts, unlikely partnerships, unconditional love, and toys who come to life. Fully realized with Pixar's knack for state-of-the-art computer animation, *Toy Story* became a watershed moment in film history—that lightning in a bottle instant where inspiration, perspiration, technology, and good old-fashioned storytelling collided, finding a perfect home in the hearts of a mass audience. The films made by Stanton and his colleagues at Pixar—*A Bug's Life*, *Monsters, Inc.*, *Finding Nemo*, *Cars*, *Wall-E*—never fail to find a spot on year-end top-ten lists, collect Oscars, and make a mint at the box office, a testament to the company's tireless work ethic and heartfelt conviction that wonder, honesty, and goodwill are the key to great stories. Stanton, a true pioneer, a movie maestro of the first order, even if you don't know his face or name, believes it's all very simple: "I make the kind of movie I want to see. That's just another way of saying, to thine own self be true." Father to two children, married for twenty years, with Best Animated Feature Oscars (one for *Finding Nemo*, the other for *Wall-E*) decorating his Mill Valley, California mantel, Stanton lives a blessed life, and he knows it. Expressing that gratitude is part of his daily practice, another way he is, indeed, true to himself.

ARRESTED DEVELOPMENT. In the art of animation, it's an asset to be in a state of arrested development. Animators tend to be Peter Pans; they are very attuned to their childhoods. We can still name every toy we ever owned, every show we ever watched, every prank we ever pulled, every imaginary friend we had. I don't know why that is, but it's how we're wired up. My outside grew up, but my insides never did, and that's the job I've got. I've never worried about making movies just for kids; I know I'm immature enough that the kids will get it, too.

HOLIDAY ROAD. Growing up, my family didn't do European vacations or fishing trips or afternoons at the ballpark. What we had was the weekend trip to the movies. We didn't even question what the movies were; we just knew we were going into a place, as a family, where stories would be told with sound and pictures and, even when the stories were not great to me, the experience always was. That's the family I came from.

(DAVID) LEAN ON ME. In addition to the films of George Lucas and Steven Spielberg, which were all coming out when I was growing up, David Lean's *Lawrence of Arabia* completely blew me away as a kid—and long before I could really understand all the nuances of its story. It's hard to ignore the scope of a film like that. You *feel* it, even if you don't completely understand it. That really set the bar for me as a storyteller.

SIT DOWN, YOU'RE ROCKIN' THE BOAT. That's what I did, musicals, all the way through junior high and high school—*Fiddler on the Roof*, *Cabaret*, *Guys and Dolls*, *Godspell*. It was the music and the storytelling I grew up on. In the late '80s, I grew to dislike that method of storytelling, because it seemed like the only way an animated film could be made— story and songs; it was the tired rubric—and it felt like animation was being put in a box. With Pixar, I really carried the flag for a long time to break that convention. Once it was broken, I was very happy to go back and revisit *Hello Dolly* from my youth—which, of course, is a key ingredient in *Wall-E*.

IT'S A WONDERFUL LIFE. When we started working on *Toy Story*, all of us at Pixar talked a lot about the elusive thing we were trying to capture with that film, and it came down to one thing: wonder. It's a rarefied element in movies. I don't believe you can fake wonder. You either sincerely arrive at it or it entirely eludes you. I don't know if we always get there, but I know we're always trying.

LOVING THE LIGHT BULB. You're going to spend four years making these movies and almost three years of that will be painful, so you need to have something to get you out of bed when everything's going wrong. For me, it's that idea that I'm in love with. Sometimes ideas need time to become attractive, and then I fall in love. *Wall-E* took some time to fall in love with, and then he took some time to grow up and move out of the house. And he done me proud.

THE RIGHT TO FIGHT. I'm working with all of my mentors and heroes and inspirations. I not only work with guys like Brad Bird and John Lasseter, absolute gods of the animation world, on par with the George Lucases and Steven Spielbergs of the filmmaking world, but I'm on a first name basis with them. Not only that, I *argue* with them.

RANDOM ACTS OF KINDNESS. When somebody shows you an act of kindness without any motivation, you're filled often with a desire to do the same thing for somebody else. I believe that happens artistically. To me, that's nirvana. If I can make a piece of art that makes someone else want to make a piece of art, then that's *it* for me. That's the goal. I'm making movies today because of all the movies I saw as a kid.

Ringo Starr

on gratitude

"We could be fighting like cats and dogs, but as soon as anyone did the count in, we did our best. Ah, you bastard, you bastard. . . . Two, three, four, boom, wacka, boom, wacka . . . and we did it. That's how it is. That's being in a band."

EIGHT YEARS IN, FORTY YEARS OUT, and tales of "Yesterday" or *Sgt. Pepper's Lonely Hearts Club Band* and *Let It Be*, are still all anyone wants to hear. Such is the albatross of Richard Starkey—née, Ringo Starr—the fourth Beatle, the lefty pounding a right-hander's drum kit, no one's favorite Beatle if you want to be snarky to Starkey. And yet, at seventy, Starr seems completely at peace with his place in the rock 'n' roll history books. Quick with a wry or self-deprecating joke or to twirl the multitude of rings on his fingers—you *do* recall from whence the stage name came, yes?—Starr knows what he knows, and what much of the world has finally figured out: In what is arguably the greatest band of all time, no one else could have done what

Ringo Starr did. What's more, while Starr may have been the last of the Beatles to embrace Eastern philosophy—famously, if disingenuously, ditching yoga camp in India because the food was too spicy and the lepers too bountiful—he's always flown the flag for peace and love, and still does with fervor. In person, Starr is quick with a quip and perfectly cast in the role of rock legend. He couldn't look *more* like a rock star, hair close-cropped, plush purple blazer, sporty mirrored shades, shoes that cost more than your refrigerator, sharper and more handsome than you'd expect, behaving like royalty—if kings and princes drew punch lines like six-shooters. When reminded of his long-ago stated ambition to "end up sort of unforgettable," Starr puts his hands atop yours and says, after a long beat for maximum effect, "I am, mate. It's come *true*!" And then he smiles, just to let you know he's joking. And that he's not. On charisma, longevity, and sheer offbeat talent, however underestimated all these years, Ringo Starr has earned his spot at any table he chooses, a poor boy from Liverpool, accident prone and frequently hospitalized, narrowly avoiding a career in dock work when his bar band found regional success and a fateful stint playing the same pub as the Beatles. The rest of everything is well-documented history, which Starr—living squarely in the present and in a place of warm gratitude—will suffer, surrender, or savor not at all. Let it be, indeed.

A HEALTHY SELF-RESPECT. I am a pop icon. I'm still in the game. People are, like, "What? You're still making music?" Yes. Because that's what I am. I'm a musician. I still like the concept of making records, hanging out with other musicians, writing with other musicians, playing, so why shouldn't I be making music?

ILL TO ILLIN'. I had this experience in the hospital when I was a child. I was sick a lot as a kid, always sick. They brought in these percussive instruments and said, "Point to the yellow dot, the tambourine hits, point to the yellow dot, the drum hits," and they gave me a drum and they came again the next week and I wouldn't play along with them unless I got the drum. That's how it started. This was the defining moment for me.

They gave me a little drum and that was it. I never wanted to play the piano or the guitar; it was always the drums for me.

78, 45, 33 1/3: HUNGRY FOR TUNES. My stepfather introduced me to a lot of music that, as a lad, I wouldn't have listened to. I was listening to the music of the day and he would say — Harry, my stepfather — "Have you heard *this*?" And it was Sarah Vaughan. "Have you heard *this*?" It was Glenn Miller. It was Billy Eckstine. It was Billy Daniels. They were his heroes, Billy Daniels and Billy Eckstine. So he introduced me to a broader range of music. I'm grateful for that.

THE BOYS IN THE BAND. There are boy bands today. There are girl bands. There are dance bands. There are corporate bands, put together by money men. Whatever. I think the bit people forget, to be in a band, you have to know each other, and you get to know each other coming up from clubs, playing free gigs, theaters, whatever, sitting in the van. That's the only way I know. You really get to know each other traveling around the country in a van together. That shows, I feel, in the Beatles' music. We could be fighting like cats and dogs, but as soon as anyone did the count in, we did our best. *Ah, you bastard, you bastard. . . . Two, three, four, boom, wacka, boom, wacka . . .* and we did it. That's how it is. *That's* being in a band.

PERFECT POP. All it takes to write the perfect pop song is luck, desire, and perseverance. (*laughs*) It's really *that* simple, mate.

GOOD MATES. The guys I play with today, we got to know each other so well that we could walk into the studio in the morning and some-one could say, "Wow, what a great day," and it's a song. All we need is a line and someone with a guitar, and we'll turn anything you say into a song. With my CD, when it's mine, it's always just twelve different ways of saying, "peace and love." I'll do that in a dozen songs, and an album we've made. It's where I'm at. You put any other four guys in a room, and they'll all write the sad song. *She's gone. . . .* (*laughs*) It's incredible. Put four guys together, and they all turn into country writers. Where's the love?

PERFECT POP, PART 2. Several songs on my recent albums, we've called them "the treadmill songs" because I work out a lot. On the treadmill, once the endorphins go, I just find it so easy to write a damned song. It just comes. All of a sudden, I'm writing a polka.

RINGO STARR, CULTURE CRITIC. The Beatles, we were "the pop group." Those other guys (the Rolling Stones) were "the rock group." I think we were a lot deeper than that, because "pop" has this connotation of fluffy in a way, and it's just there for the summer and then it's going to go. I think we proved that wrong. But what do I know? I'm over twenty-one, and it's always harder when you're over twenty-one.

YESTERDAY. If you listen to what's out now, it rarely sounds modern and then you listen to some stuff, and you go, "Well, there goes *that* band again." I'm always looking for the perfect marriage between nostalgia and modernity, with a lot of love and gratitude. I think I always have. That's the thing *I* do.

THE SECRET O' LIFE. I heard a great line recently by Carl Jung. He was being interviewed when he was, like, 300 years old. His family was ministers and church people. At the end of the interview on this old BBC show, they said, "Well, do you believe in God?" And he said, "No. I *know*." And it stuck with me so hard. How beautiful was that? "I *know*." Well . . . okay then . . . .

ALL THINGS CONSIDERED. Those old songs, they're still out there, like new every time I hear them. But for me, I think "Photograph" is one of the finest songs I wrote. I wrote it in Spain on the guitar, with my three chords and my words. I came back to London and gave it to George Harrison who put in the other ten chords. (*laughs*) I wasn't very good at finishing songs. And George, he was always trying to put Krishna into the songs. That's how we were. We were young. Was it for the best? I don't know, mate. Peace and love, right? Peace and love.

Danielle Steel

on gratitude

"Without their words, I am useless.
So I am grateful to all writers."

IT WOULD BE TOO EASY to say that Danielle Steel lives the stories she tells, and yet it also wouldn't be entirely untrue. Steel has penned more than 100 novels, which have sold in excess of 600 million copies worldwide, securing a virtual stronghold on the *New York Times* bestseller list for more than three decades. These works of fiction—from *No Greater Love* to *Sisters*, *Going Home* to *Passion's Promise*—tend to draw on the epic, succulent details of Steel's private life: the exotic, international upbringing, the five marriages to wildly memorable men (a millionaire, a heroin addict, an incarcerated serial rapist, and an acclaimed vintner among them), the bevy of "yours, mine, and ours" children, the sudden shocks, personal tragedies, and virtually unprecedented commercial success. Yes, that would be Danielle Steel, the seventh bestselling novelist *of all time*. And yet, in real life, Danielle Steel is far more than a

Danielle Steel heroine. Born in 1947, now residing in a fifty-five-room San Francisco mansion built 100 years ago by sugar tycoon Adolph B. Spreckels, Steel has found and embraced an elegance, grace, and compassion that oftentimes escapes her protagonists, even the ones afforded the happiest of endings. Between penning impossibly success-ful books on a disciplined schedule, a necessity of meeting publishing deadlines, she has raised nearly a dozen children over the years. Steel also spends a good deal of time supporting local artists, harkening to her early years as a fashion designer and aspiring artist herself, and raising funds and awareness for the Nick Traina Foundation, named for her son, who took his own life in 1997 as a result of bipolar disorder and drug abuse. Professionally speaking, Steel clearly has the Midas touch. Personally, Steel devotes time every day to counting her blessings, even when the minutes are unforgiving and the days are teeming with plot twists ripped from the pages of her own powerhouse imagination.

THE REAL STORY. I think my books appeal to people because they're so real. The feelings in these books are autobiographical, even if the storylines usually aren't. I've written more than a hundred books. Even *I've* run out of life experiences. It's like being an actor—you throw yourself into the role with the feelings you've had in your life. I can ani-mate the situations I create with the life I've had. And I think people feel the honesty in that.

HARD TIMES ARE COLORBLIND. People sometimes have the sense that success or money or fame prevents the hard things from hap-pening to you. That's what my books are about. If you're human, no matter your station, you are never exempt from tragedy, and you always have to find a way back to your feet. Remembering that is a real blessing.

WOMAN OF STEEL. I publish three books a year, and it takes me two and a half years to write each one. I work on anywhere from three to five books at a time. I sleep very little, and I have no life. (*laughs*) It's very simple. And I love it. When my kids were small, I worked when they were in school or sleeping. Now I work all the time, and I do it like a painter who might have five canvasses going at the same time in different studios. The work ethic is simple: I told myself a long time ago—if you don't put your behind in that chair, you'll have to put it in someone else's chair. That settled that.

THE OFFSPRING. Parenting is the most important job of my life— my greatest accomplishment and my greatest joy. I totally forgot they'd grow up and be gone, I was so busy shuttling between the soccer matches and the orthodontist and snuggling with them. It goes so fast. Of course, there are always challenges. I lost my son (Nicholas Traina) in 1997, and he was—and still is—an enormous blessing. Since his death, I've established two foundations in his name, and we've been able to help thousands of people suffering with mental illness. That help has made a difference in the world, and that, also, is a blessing. That's one of the ways children—even in the heartbreak—can be a real blessing.

COLOR MY WORLD. My training is in design, and I had a gallery for four years in San Francisco, and now I'm guest curating in some local galleries. I love working with emerging artists and helping them. It's so exciting. The visual arts always have been such an important part of my life. I still do a fair amount of interior design, and it's so wonderful, instead of describing something on the page and hoping they see what you see, to actually make it happen. That's the power of the visual arts. It also tends to happen much more quickly than a book.

JOIE DE VIVRE. My parents were European, and so I spent a lot of my youth in Europe and then in New York, too. I'm more European in style and philosophy, but I've been a United States transplant all my life. In America, I've always felt slightly out of step, but in Europe now, they remind me that I've been an American more than half my life, and it's affected the way I think. (*laughs*) It gives you a greater breadth in your thinking to live in two different worlds. Sometimes it's confusing as to where you belong, but it's definitely opened more doors for me, and it's allowed me to live a different kind of life.

THE DEDICATION PAGE. I'm very grateful for the long-term support of my readers, the pleasure they take in my books, and the generous way they express that to me. They are the unseen force in my life—people I've not met, for the most part, but who drive me and inspire me and move me deeply to always do better work.

John Updike

on gratitude

"I wanted to give the mundane its beautiful due."

RABBIT WAS FINALLY AT REST, January 27, 2009, with the passing of John Updike, America's "last true man of letters," according to the *New York Times*. The majority of American postwar authors—from Roth to DeLillo, Pynchon to Mailer—grew sweaty carving new rules on a postmodern playground. They wrestled with a pugilist's intensity and a poet's tongue regarding the fragmentation of time, the dislocation of contemporary man, the onslaught of technology, and the crisis of representation. Updike, however, refused to do battle. Instead, Updike—a Pennsylvania boy, class president, covaledictorian, full scholarship student at Harvard, and a *New Yorker* contributor starting when he was in his early twenties—put on his cardigans, chomped a pipe, and told more traditional stories through more traditional means, penning books of quiet genius, like the Pulitzer Prize-winning Rabbit Angstrom tetralogy, *Couples*, *The Centaur*, *The Witches of Eastwick*, along with volumes of poetry and some of the greatest literary and art criticism of the last century. With nostalgia, reverence, and a deep appreciation, Updike wrote of suburbia, the middle, the mainstream, believing that's where extremes were most likely to collide. Updike's literary alter ego, Rabbit Angstrom, was an average American male, struggling with issues of abandonment, fear, obsolescence, and redemption, his journey elegantly set against four decades of tumultuous U.S. history. This was Updike's milieu, and purposefully. "Life as it is lived by most people, those that I knew certainly, was worthy of artistic intention. I've always wanted to honor normal life — full as it is with magic and surprises — in literature," he says. "I wanted to give the mundane its beautiful due." Updike was a literary realist, employing a sensual, occasionally esoteric vocabulary and a powerful authorial voice in an era where narrators — and their accounts — were highly suspect. Updike didn't require postmodern tricks and tropes to be brilliant; his voice was more than enough. In fact, Updike might have been the only storyteller in the late twentieth century whom you could actually trust or bring home for dinner. In our conversation just a few months before he succumbed to lung cancer, Updike was gentle, playful, serene — the smartest man in any room, and elegant in every way. If he knew he was dying, his discourse and demeanor never revealed the fact. He was a portrait of grace, giving seventy-six years of gratitude its beautiful due.

MY MAMA SAYS. I grew up watching her at her little typewriter, a small Remington as I remember, clacking away, a Cornell graduate, sending off stories to magazines, then getting them back in a couple of weeks. So the routine of becoming a writer was familiar to me. I owe my career, really, to her and her example of making a go of it in this strange trade.

CRACK YOUR OWN WHIP. Whether you have a boss or, like me, you have to be your own boss, you have to have discipline in this life. I do. I've kept the same writing schedule for fifty years.

THE HUMBLE WORDSMITH. I'm not a movie star or a rock star. I maybe get two or three letters a week out of the blue, for some reason, and as I'm an old guy now, most of the letters are kindly. They do keep you going. This is an unsponsored job. I don't get paid without readers. So I appreciate that enduring fan base. It does keep me going. And for someone to take the time to say they like me. That's a blessing.

ONCE A VALEDICTORIAN. I'm a Pennsylvania high school boy, who got to love good report cards and awards, and I've had, I think I can say, my share. But for every award you win, there are dozens you don't. In a sense, the net pleasure of award winning is almost balanced out by the irritation of not winning every single one. (*laughs*) I wouldn't say no to the Nobel, but I'm not sure my writing has been, at any point, arresting enough to capture their attention.

THE PLACE THAT YOU CALL HOME. The place you grow up and spend your first twenty years is a measure of every place, in some way. The impressions are deeper and warmer and, for me, they are drawn not only in the Rabbit books, but in a lot of my work. My upbringing and impressions are everywhere alive in my work.

FUNNY BONES. To sit and hold a page and laugh out loud struck me as a remarkable enactment of the immaterial upon the material—to reach out and get a reader to laugh is a high achievement and a life-enhancing one, and doesn't do any harm, as far as I can tell. I believe humor is every bit as noble as drama, and just as honest.

ELBOW GREASE. Those that were born in the Depression era, as I was, were born on the low end of the demographic. We learned to make much of what we had and to make due and to work hard. That sense of working was very much around in the Depression. Children got the idea, too, that the good life was had in working and working hard. It's worth remembering that today.

THE KINDNESS OF STRANGERS. The nice thing about fiction is it develops our ability to empathize. How easily the mind takes you to the mind of an eighteen-year-old girl in eighteenth-century Russia, for example. Literature makes us more human. That empathy is a healthy effect of reading and writing fiction. More people should do it.

Kurt Vonnegut
on gratitude

*"Simplicity and sincerity, two
things I am grateful for."*

KURT VONNEGUT was doing the Lord's work, whether you believe in God or not, and Vonnegut didn't. In more than a dozen books, including *Slaughterhouse-Five*, *Cat's Cradle*, *Mother Night*, and *Timequake*, the great American author—arguably *the* great American author—combined gallows humor, satire, and science fiction with a deep and abiding humanism. Precious few authors have ever loved humankind so completely and unromantically; Vonnegut saw us for who we really are, and loved us anyway. His work, unflinchingly brutal at times, hilariously brittle, wildly imaginative, and always easy to read, sometimes even dotted with crude line drawings, implored us to smile on our brothers and love one another right now, to be kind and decent and honest—and even noble. Vonnegut always asked us to be the very best we could be, and he refused to give up his stranglehold on our funny bone along the way. These are things for which we should all be grateful. Each of the four conversations shared with Vonnegut between October 2000 and March 6, 2007, one month before his passing at the age of eighty-four, virtually teemed with the subject of gratitude. Jazz, fatherhood, dancing, sacrifice, comedy, ordinary heroes, friendship, brotherhood, the creative process . . . these were all things Vonnegut counted as great blessings in his life, punctuated often with a hacksaw laugh, the result of chain-smoking Pall Mall cigarettes since his teenage years, each moment expressed with pitch-perfect timing, the heart of a teacher, and a prophet's wistful assuredness. It is perhaps instructive that a man can fight in World War II, survive the infamous Dresden bombing, the sudden loss of friends, wives, and countless loved ones, not to mention the last two decades of American history, and still believe that "everything was beautiful and nothing hurt," which he scrawled onto an illustration of a tombstone a few years before his death, probably laughing all the while. God bless you, Mr. Vonnegut, wherever you are, and thank *you* for everything.

SLAPSTICK OF ANOTHER KIND. The world is too serious. To get mad at a work of art—because maybe somebody, somewhere is blowing his stack over what I've done—is like getting mad at a hot fudge sundae. I say, *be* silly.

RAISON D'ETRE. I tell everybody to practice some art, no matter how badly or how well. It doesn't matter. It's the experience of becoming—of creating—that truly matters. It is as important as sex or food. It's a tragedy to me that our schools have cut art out of the curriculum, because (they say) it's not a way to make a living. Well, it's *not* a way to make a living; it's a way to *become*, to find out what you are, what you can do, what's inside of you. And that's enough.

THE SIDEWAYS WORLD. Joseph Heller and I were very good friends, and quite unlike each other, at least as writers. I miss him today. What Joe said is, if it hadn't been for World War II, he would've been in the dry-cleaning business. If it hadn't been for World War II, I'd now be a gardener at (my hometown paper) the *Indianapolis Star.*

TO THE POINT. I've said it before: I write in the voice of a child. That makes me readable in high school. Simple sentences have always served me well. And I don't use semicolons. It's hard to read anyway, especially for high school kids. Also, I avoid irony. I don't like people saying one thing and meaning the other. Simplicity and sincerity, two things I am grateful for.

CALL TO ACTION. To stare at horizontal lines of phonetic symbols and Arabic numbers and to be able to put a show on in your head, it requires the reader to perform. If you can do it, you can go whaling in the South Pacific with Herman Melville, or you can watch Madame Bovary make a mess of her life in Paris. With pictures and movies, all you have to do is sit there and look at them and it happens to you. I am grateful to people who still concern themselves with the work of being readers.

BREVITY'S RAINBOW. Look, it's perfectly okay to be influential for a short time. There are many writers who succeeded quite well at not wasting people's time, if only for a short time. And then maybe that peters out. That's all right. It's nice to be useful for six to ten minutes sometimes, say, in a fire. Or: I went out on a date with a nice girl, and it went awfully well. Gee, that was a swell five hours. It doesn't have to last forever.

WHATEVER GETS YOU THROUGH THE NIGHT. I asked my son Mark what he thought life was all about, and he said, "We are here to help each other get through this thing, whatever it is." I think that says it best. You can do that as a comedian, a writer, a painter, a musician. He's a pediatrician. There are all kinds of ways we can help each other get through today. There are some things that help. Musicians really do it for me. I wish I were one, because they help a lot. They help us get through a couple hours.

THE PERFECT DAY. I think it would be the moment where I was doing everything right, where I was beyond criticism. It was back in World War II. It was snowing, but everything was black. The trucks were rolling in. I was surrounded by my buddies. And my rifle was between my knees, my helmet on my head. I was ready for anything. And I was right where I belonged. That would be the moment. It would *have* to be the moment.

MISSION ACCOMPLISHED. At eighty-four, I feel that I've done everything I can do. Please can't I go home now? That's what I felt after the second world war: Please, can I go home now? And I think about where home was, and where I would like to go. Indianapolis when I was nine-years-old, and I had a brother and a sister and a cat and a dog and a father and a mother, aunts, uncles, cousins. I had a tribe out there in Indianapolis, which no longer exists. Everybody should have one. I'm happy that I did.

Forest Whitaker
on gratitude

"Any chance you have to see the world through someone else's eyes is always a gift. It allows you to live your own life more clearly."

PAST ACTION BRINGS CONSEQUENCES, according to some schools of thought. If you're an actor, your deeds, noble or nefarious, provide your back story, your motivation, the road map to your here and now. If you're spiritually inclined, what you've done, or not done, creates karma, good and bad, which must be relieved and released through the living of multiple lives, each incarnation a calm, continued quest toward pure liberation. If you're Forest Whitaker, the Oscar-winning actor, the two concepts are inseparable, equally true and in perfect harmony today on his life's path. In his work, as in his life, Whitaker does not go to the light; he brings it with him. Whether he is portraying a heroin-addled jazz icon, a charismatic, hair-trigger third world dictator, a blissed-out Mafia hit man, or a soul-shattered crime-scene investigator, Whitaker goes deep. He isolates the precise location of his characters' humanity, even in the vilest of creatures, showing audiences exactly where these men most need to be loved, or, at least, accepted. This illumination is essential for audiences, he says. But also, for himself: "That's why you'll find that I make creative choices that are very different from each other, that might not look like they make sense. It's because I'm living my journey and trying to grow and continue with my awakening and awareness," he says. Born in 1961 to a blue-collar family in Texas, the young and physically imposing Whitaker had NFL dreams that were well within his grasp until a devastating back injury required a sudden shift of gears. Surprising to many was the golden operatic tenor the all-league defensive tackle had been concealing, a gift he honed at University of Southern California's music conservatory. (Whitaker also studied at USC's drama conservatory.) Upon graduation, Whitaker went straight to work for a veritable who's-who of filmmaking geniuses, from Cameron Crowe (*Fast Times at Ridgemont High*) to Martin Scorsese (*The Color of Money*), Barry Levinson (*Good Morning, Vietnam*) to Oliver Stone (*Platoon*), as well as Robert Altman, Neil Jordan, Jim Jarmusch, Clint Eastwood, and Wayne Wang. Whitaker's work has always been soulful, sublime. "Transcendent" is a word that appears in no fewer than 200 film reviews of his work. A longtime vegetarian, yogi, and avid meditator, Whitaker is soft-spoken, intensely mindful, someone who hears not only your words but the sounds they make and the intentions behind them. Married with four children, and enjoying a successful run on CBS's recently launched *CSI: Crime Scene Investigation* spinoff, Whitaker lives a life of charity, compassion, and kindness, spreading grace with all he encounters—be they friends, family, strangers—or even the villains and heroes he plays. "We're all completely connected," he says. "I'm connected to the characters I play. I *know* that's the truth."

LITTLE WONDERS. I think each day is its own blessing, really. Life is so much about seeing the small things.

HOW COMPASSION HAPPENS. In this life, my work has allowed me to be and see places where the polarity and duality of things are everywhere evident—the jungles of the world, where people are living, literally, in the mud to the palaces of kings and all of the emotion and ideas and ideologies between them. These are all gifts—any chance you have to see the world through someone else's eyes is always a gift. It allows you to live your own life more clearly.

THE GIVING TREE. I spent my summers on my grandparents' farm in Texas, and my grandfather, in particular, taught me so much. He put a seed in the palm of my hand once and didn't say much about it. But I came to see the blessing of what a seed is, what it takes to be nurtured, to plant it, to protect it, to keep it in harmony with the elements, with the sun, the vermin, and to help it to realize its deep space of potentiality. My grandfather taught me all of that, without ever saying much. I think that lesson has informed everything about me.

MY MAMA SAYS. My mother taught me that I didn't have to believe in the things she believed in, so long as I believed in something bigger than myself. That's one of the biggest things anyone has ever told me. This is a powerful gift. We are all connected to something. You can call it whatever you want.

NOTE BY NOTE. Music, because it's vibration, it literally moves your heart and moves your mind. The sounds move you, not just your feelings, but everything about you. It's energy. For me, when I was singing, it was a pure expression of spirit—the best one I had found up to that point. I did musicals, like *Cabaret* and *Jesus Christ Superstar*, and opera and art songs, light arias, everything I could. Music has always been a pointer, bringing me to self-expression. It led me to acting which, for me, is an even greater form of self-expression.

COMMON SOURCE. My goal as an actor has always been to find the connecting piece—the light, the illumination each character has with me, which means that it also connects somehow with everyone else, because we all are really connected. That's always been the goal. Great art does that. It reminds us that we're all connected, which means we're never lonely. The breadth of characters I've played and stories I've told have been a reflection of that, and they've allowed me to speak directly to people I've known and people I haven't. The goal has never changed: It's always been about connection. Acting has allowed me to do that.

IT IS WHAT IT IS, AND IT ALL BELONGS. When I was starting off as an actor, I was having trouble with my characters. I was having trouble playing the characters "right." I felt like a part of me was always sticking out in the work, like I was protruding or getting in the way. And my godfather said, "What makes you think that's not exactly how they are, or that this isn't all completely real? What makes you think the story you're telling doesn't exist in that moment? You have to see it all in the moment, in the moment, in the moment." It resonated for me in my work at that time. I had been frustrated, but I've become a better observer and more attuned.

LEARNING TO BREATHE. I had meditated for years before doing *Ghost Dog* (with Jim Jarmusch), but during that film I meditated deeply. I meditated three hours a day, sometimes, before I'd work, to find that space for that character. At this point in my life, I don't divorce my spiritual life from my work. My work is a way to explore and connect and grow as a being.

A ROSE BY ANY OTHER NAME. My name is my father's name and my grandfather's, too. My children are Ocean and Sonnet and True and Autumn. My son, I wanted him to have a greater berth than me, to have a vibration that was larger than mine so he could have a different start in the world. I wanted him to have a vastness, so I called him Ocean. Sonnet, my daughter, we were thinking about the poetry of life and music and the world. These children, they really are like their names. It's amazing. Naming your children, it's a way of laying a hint of destiny on them.

THE CHARITABLE WARRIOR. I get more from giving than from anything else in my life. Anytime you can be taught, that's powerful. Anytime you can teach what you've been taught, that's powerful, too. These are small reminders of how we are connected. I was in Uganda a few years ago (making *The Last King of Scotland*, for which he won an Academy Award for Best Actor) and there was this child soldier following us around everywhere. He'd been a soldier his entire life. He'd been made to kill people. He'd been made to kill his parents. He'd been at war. And the guide that was with me said that this child had just begun to smile, just since we'd been there. Only just. This child danced and talked with me and put down his gun and shared his life instead of sacrificing it. And it made him smile. That is one of the best gifts I've ever received.

Steven Wright

on gratitude

*"I don't know how I got
like that, but I'm happy that my
brain is this way."*

THERE IS A JOKE, AND IT GOES LIKE THIS: Two Buddhist monks sit side by side overlooking a forest on a lovely afternoon. No words are exchanged between them. Nothing much happens. The wind is still. The forest does not move. Hours later, one of the monks begins to laugh. The other monk looks inquisitively at his partner. "Look!" says the laughing monk. "The *trees!*" End joke. Granted, no one's bound to die laughing at this funny business, but it does illustrate quite exactly where lies the genius of comedian Steven Wright whose deadpan, monotone quips and observations, adored by fans of the stand-up art form for three decades, reveal such careful witness to life itself that one can see in them the forest *and* the trees, the reality and the utter absurdity with which it is represented in our words, thoughts, and feelings—not to mention the constant movement of our imaginations. Only three-year-olds point out how completely, sublimely ridiculous—or miraculous—life is with less attachment to the outcome of their observations. You often get the sense watching Wright perform, words slowly dripping from his mouth like honey at a temperature below zero, with all the arc and intonation of a yardstick, that he's not even making jokes. In the world according to Steven Wright, anarchy is not a means to an end, literalism is not an act of defiance, and the bon mot is not a tool of seduction; it's simply a way to see the world. *His* way. "It's a small world," says Wright, "but I wouldn't want to paint it." It's perfect logic, to be sure, and also really damn funny. His *Tonight Show* debut a lifetime ago in 1982, Wright remains a singular voice in the world of comedy, virtually impossible to imitate. For his efforts, the New York native has won a Grammy and an Oscar, the latter for the 1988 short film, *The Appointments of Dennis Jennings*. In conversation, Wright reveals an artist at work, a gentle, inquiring mind, a shyness that almost steals the alphabet from his memory at times, a deep appreciation for the life he's lived and, in the one moment of unfiltered ebullience, an abiding love for baseball and the Boston Red Sox, specifically. There is no persona in the Steven Wright universe, just one man and his beautiful mind.

BRAIN DONOR. I don't know how I got like that, but I'm happy that my brain is this way. I am grateful for my imagination. Some of it I was just born with, but also you have to use your imagination. You have to notice things in life. You have to see stuff. From the time I wake up to the time I go to sleep, I'm bombarded by thousands of pieces of information—a sign or a word or a book, or some conversation I had or overheard, something on the street. And then my mind makes some of that stuff into jokes. That's what I do.

BILL OF HEALTH. I don't like being sick. I'm not usually sick. I'm glad about that.

FEAR OF FLYING. Nobody likes public speaking, but I was a really introverted, shy guy. When I thought of doing this job, I never thought, "How am I going to do that being so introverted?" I was just watching Johnny Carson all the time and wanted to do the thing that George Carlin and David Brenner and Robert Klein were doing. That looked like a good goal. I thought it would be cool. And then I had to force myself on stage every single time to see if I could do this goal I had. The conflict was very intense. *You've got to go on. I don't want to go on.* But I kept doing it over and over. I would say it took a couple of years to get anywhere near relaxed. Even now, it's still an intense thing to go out on stage. It's not like talking to someone in my living room. I'm grateful I kept trying.

CLASSICS ROCK. Music is one of the amazing things about life. I love music. My favorites are the Beatles and Bob Dylan and Neil Young, stuff from that time. I like Cowboy Junkies, too. I love seeing live music.

STILL LIFE. Drawing and painting is my first creative thing. I started doing that in elementary school, and I took some classes in high school. I was painting way before I did comedy. It helps me do the comedy, I think. I used to paint realistically. When you do that, you notice details in things that you wouldn't normally notice. If there was a wine bottle on a table next to a vase, you'd notice the wine bottle and you'd notice the vase. But you'd also notice the shape of the space between those two things. I think that somehow influenced how I viewed the world. When I went to write comedy, I was noticing those kinds of things.

GOD BLESS YOU, MR. VONNEGUT. I'm grateful for Kurt Vonnegut. He's my literary hero. I've read all of his books—some of them many times. I'm grateful for his mind. Reading him makes my imagination go. He was just amazing. I got to meet him and spend time with him, so I'm grateful for that, too. We spent years talking about writing something together, back when I lived in New York, but we never did. He was really a nice guy—and different. I liked that about him.

BAGGING OSCAR. I won an Academy Award, like, twenty years ago, which was cool. I'm grateful for that. Mine still looks the same, but my friend, the director of the film also won one that night, and he says his is changing color a little bit. The day after I won, I had to fly back to New York. I had the thing wrapped up in a plastic trash bag inside my carry-on luggage and I was going through airport security. They had me open it up, and I took it out. They just looked at it for a minute and then I just put it back in the bag. That was it. They didn't comment. They didn't say anything. They didn't ask me what I won it for. They must have known what it was. But they were very quiet.

BLEEDING RED. Baseball is one of my favorite things in my life. I love the park. I love the connection to the team, the connection to the other people rooting for the team. It's almost like a tribal thing. You're all connected. You feel like everybody knows everybody. I'm always glad when the season starts. I've been a Red Sox fan my whole life, even though I'm from New York.

ALL YOU NEED IS LOVE. I have some really very caring, creative friends in my life. I've accumulated them over my lifetime, and I'm grateful for them. I'm grateful for my brothers and my sister and my father, when he was alive. And I'm grateful for my mother. She's such a character. She's really intense, but that's not it. She can be funny. I don't know how to describe it, but you can feel how much she cares about you. I don't want to break it down more than that.

You
on gratitude

Your gratitude could very well
change someone else's life.

It's your turn now.

You don't have to be rich or famous for gratitude to matter. It's important to count your blessings, and to share them with others, no matter your station in life. One of the key purposes of this book and the accompanying movement I've dubbed The Thanksgiving Project is to connect readers around the world with their own personal stories of gratitude. So please, *please,* take a moment today—and then tomorrow, and every day following—to look at your life and write down one thing—*at least* one thing—for which you are grateful. Then share it with someone. Share it with me! *todd@thegratitudelist.org.* Your gratitude could very well change someone else's life.

Don't know where to start with gratitude? That's easy. It's about being in touch with your senses. Start with what you're feeling. What is your body *feeling*? Where are your toes? What's at your fingertips? Do you notice that rise and fall at your core? Embrace that breath. That's a first, and fairly reliable, clue that you're alive. (This is always a good place to start. Alive? Check!)

Then tune into what you're hearing. I don't know your particular aural landscape: It could be crickets in the meadows or the El screeching apocalypse outside your apartment window, an adagio rehearsed before curtain or someone else's baby insisting on a clean diaper. Perhaps it's even silence. But there is a rhythm to all that we hear.

Do the same with your sight and your smell and your taste. Really experience it all. And remember: Even the things that don't please you, the things you think are painful, they usually make great stories—especially if you remember that they're *only* stories.

Your senses are the keys to your gratitude. If you're not feeling your life, not open to it and to really *experiencing* it, then you're not connecting. Instead, try to be here, now.

Get started by answering these questions:

- Who gave you life?

- Who encouraged you to keep living?

- What flavors do you love?

- What film or book or song changed your life? How? Why?

- What's that thing that person told you that stopped your mind?

- Can you recall or describe what would be your perfect day?

- What is the best gift you've ever received?

- Who was your favorite teacher or mentor, and why?

- Describe the most amazing moment from your favorite vacation.

- What is the most memorable advice you've ever been given—even if it was horrible advice you were smart enough to ignore?

- Try to recall the moment when you realized you were more powerful or capable than you thought. How did that feel?

- Describe a moment in which you felt smaller than you were, but were elevated by faith or friendship.

- What is the smallest, most trivial thing for which you are grateful?

Remember to share your gratitude lists at *www.thegratitudelist.org*. We're listening. . . . While you're at the website, please take a moment to investigate other ways in which you can make a difference in this world. Give a little time, a little love, whatever you can. Generosity is often the first small step toward living more abundantly yourself. Every one of us can change the world. Everything is possible. And little by little, we'll help each other through this thing, as Vonnegut said, whatever it is. That's our pleasure and our privilege, and it begins right now.

acknowledgments

Sure, all things are always possible and, as at least one friend in this book suggests "ordinary people change the world," but not without a lot of love, light, and support. The interesting thing is, compiling this list, I see how interconnected everyone on it really is, how we really *are* all in this together. This means *On Gratitude* belongs to you and to them as much as it came from my own fingertips.

Mom, without you I am not born, and Dad, without you, I do not know what a good man is, nor the glory of Rodgers and Hammerstein and the power of make-believe. Matthew, you've carried me and taught me more than you know, and Bronwen, you make my brother an even better man. Glo, without you, I honestly don't know that I'd be who I am today. Thanks for slipping me *Garp* when I was twelve; it changed my life, even if I no longer believe we are all terminal cases. Lloyd, Nancy, Opal, and Herman, my grandparents, whose influence and generosity still resonate so deeply through so many lives, not least of all my own. Elaine, thanks for the typewriter, and G, thanks for all of it—it was necessary and important. So many great, life-changing teachers: Dorie Beaumont,

Jerry Perreau, Steve Campbell, Mary Rago, and Les Abramson, how I miss you and your snail tattoo. Travel light, right?

Thanks, also, to the three reporters who made me want to be a journalist: Kermit the Frog, Clark Kent, and Richie Cunningham. No joke. Porter, you scoundrel, your faith has always elevated me, and I thank you for it. Mr. Meltzer, Mr. Johnston, and James Morrison, three of the many genuine gentlemen I've met along this path, thank you beyond all words for your kindness and faith. There is good work ahead of us, I am sure. Michael, Ryan, Eric, Phil, Kevin, Guy, Swampy, Josh, Greg, Sandy, and all of my brothers, we are almost enough to play nine innings, which makes me a very blessed man. (By the way, Guy, your book's next. The world awaits. . . .) The Pirates, Kings, and Warriors, I didn't know I had it in me; thanks for allowing me the room to learn how to win often and lose gracefully. Uncle Jim, Reverend Kelly, my brother, hopefully Chris Nolan will become more prolific; other-wise, we'll just have to find a senseless hobby like other dudes. I love you. And to all of the Kelly-Gordon-Platt brigade—Barbara, Elliot, Maryjane, Angie, Kaitlyn, Ken, Rick, John, Jason, Kenny, Bonnie, and all of the lovely littles—thank you for offering such open arms as I whistle along this pathway. I am grateful. Lorelei, you reminded me of my riches when I felt most broke, and I thank you for that. Susy, thank you for your grace, your gifted eye, and making me look as interesting and handsome as humanly possible; no easy feat. Shellen and Crisann, who dream twice as hard and do thrice as big, thank you for casting your genius in my general direction, and your kindness too. Thanks to the Lewis Family for the safe haven in which to do this typing. I honestly don't know how this book would have happened without the four walls of Silver Strand and your extraordinary hospitality. Dyann, Jessica, Karen, and all of the beautiful souls in our community, it really does take a village, and I am so grateful to be held in yours—even if it is as the town clown.

So many great editors have helped me pay the rent through the years by considering me a go-to writer: Hogan, O'Brien, Dezuzio, Davis, Vasiloff, Poole, Hockensmith, Cope, Darling, Ponder, Jones, Marsh. I appreciate the opportunity to contribute to your publications. Christy and the Yoga Blend family, you illuminated this path for me, allowed me to simply be who I am, no matter how imperfect I felt, and to Gurmukh, Tej, the Blue Jetha, and the Goldenbridge gang, who showed me how deep the journey goes. And to The Yogi Tree brigade, teachers and students alike, you are perfect just as you are, and my life is so much the richer for your love and light. Thank you for that.

Thanks, too, to the kind hearts at Shambhala Meditation Center in Eagle Rock, who teach me, still, how to dance in the rain.

Lucinda, you are a rock star, the best traveling companion a first-time author could ever hope for. Thanks for clearing the road and lighting the way, always above and beyond. Thanks to the family at Adams Media for providing the paper and the ink and the glue and the belief that this book could actually matter. To every single person included in this book, an enormous thanks. If this book touches just one life, it is only because of the beauty you have offered. My work was always and only getting out of the way and listening to *you.*

Children, children, children: Aidan, Julian, Hunter, Kody, Joanna, Javera, Ashley, Jacob, Isaiah . . . this life is unimaginable without you. This book was only born, in some small part, when each of you was, and when our paths first crossed, for that's when my own gratitude took root and blossomed. I love you all with every beat of my heart, and thank you for always insisting I be a better man. And to the coach's wife, beautiful lover, you daisy-picking dreamer, you always knew I could, and loved me when I didn't believe you, and love me just the same now that I do. Thank you for that. It's what I always needed.

And you, yes *you*, thank you for holding this book in your hands. The journey begins right now. What are you grateful for? We're listening. . . .

Portions of interviews contained within *On Gratitude* were previously published in the following outlets:

Spirit Magazine
Kristen Bell
Jeff Bridges
Alton Brown
Roger Ebert
Jonathan Safran Foer
Morgan Freeman
Dave Grohl
B. B. King
Sir Ben Kingsley
John Krasinski
Joel McHale
Dolly Parton
Zachary Quinto
Maya Rudolph
Andrew Stanton
Danielle Steel
John Updike
Forest Whitaker

US Airways Magazine
Francis Ford Coppola
Marcia Gay Harden
Dean Koontz
Liev Schreiber
Ringo Starr
Kurt Vonnegut

American Way Magazine
Ray Bradbury
Ricky Gervais

Samuel L. Jackson
Hugh Laurie
Annie Liebovitz

Pages Magazine (now defunct)
Nikki Giovanni
Joyce Carol Oates
Anne Rice

Mean Magazine (now defunct)
David Lynch
Seth MacFarlane

Geek Monthly (now defunct)
Seth Rogen

praise for *On Gratitude*

"This book smashes the myth of the self-absorbed celebrity. Jensen's inspiring collection of interviews is testimony to the power of gratitude to heal, to energize, and to change lives. Through the lens of gratefulness he offers us a previously unexplored glimpse into the private lives of these public figures."

—Dr. Robert A. Emmons, author of
Thanks! How Practicing Gratitude Can Make You Happier

"Having an attitude of gratitude is good for our body, minds, and spirits. May this book inspire you to practice daily!"
—MJ Ryan, author of *Attitudes of Gratitude* and *A Grateful Heart*

"Todd Aaron Jensen has interviewed icons in the fields of music, literature, and film—everyone a giant in their fields—all joined by one shared truth: that the only sure path to fulfillment is through gratitude. I am grateful for Todd's leadership in this movement which has the power to transform lives and the world."
—Nina Lesowitz, author of *Living Life as a Thank You*, and *The Courage Companion: Living Life with True Power*

"I was deeply touched by the honesty and open-hearted sharing of these powerful cultural icons. These stories are thoughtful. They are uplifting. Many of them are quite funny. In other words, they are so deeply human—a way for every reader to feel more completely connected to his brothers and sisters on this planet. I appreciate your writing this beautiful book on this great subject for all of humanity at this time."
—Gurmukh Kaur Khalsa, owner, Goldenbridge Yoga, bestselling author of *The Eight Human Talents: The Yoga Way to Restore the Balance and Serenity Within You*

"This compilation goes beyond lists of favorite things. *On Gratitude* highlights the meaning and joy in each person's life, from the presence of

family and friends, to great books, music, and films, to personal accomplishments. Reading this book made me smile and uplifted my spirit."
— Ronlyn Domingue, author of *The Mercy of Thin Air*

"A can't-put-down book filled with sparking golden nuggets that will breathtakingly stop you in your reading; prompting you to ponder, to reflect, to remember, to find new heroes and remember gratitude. Each chapter is filled with introductions and interviews with remarkable people, reminding you, the reader, that you, too, are remarkable and worthy to share on gratitude. We are all listening."
— Sumner M. Davenport; keynote speaker, bounce-back expert,
bestselling author, *The "G" Spot: The Ecstasy of Live Through Gratitude* and
Stress Out: Show Stress Who's the Boss

"I'm so grateful for *On Gratitude*. It's wonderful to read the thoughts and hopes of some of the people I most admire — and just plain love — on the planet. The stories are smart, pithy, and filled with wonderful observations on and advice about art, work, family, the world, and life that I will surely use. What a fun read!"
— Lisa See, author of *Shanghai Girls*, *Peony in Love*,
and *Snow Flower and the Secret Fan*

"Those of us who are blessed to know Todd Jensen appreciate him as both seeker and creator of truth. One of his greatest joys is to help us recognize the seeker in ourselves and help us become the creator of what we seek. When he sees that truth revealed, his gratitude is contagious. As you take pleasure in Todd's greatest joy as it is revealed within this book, you will find yourself, too. And you will be glad for it and comforted by it, and you will be grateful for the discovery."
— James Morrison, actor/filmmaker and yoga instructor

"Todd Aaron Jensen's *On Gratitude* is a delightful and inspiring labor of love by an experienced writer. Like *Chicken Soup for the Soul*, Jensen's labor of love will touch your heart and compel you to look always on the bright side. Hearing from many voices, some famous and some not, will make you want to pick this book up and never put it down, all the time wanting to thank the author for his hard work and imaginative interviewing skills."

—Selden Edwards, bestselling author of *The Little Book*

"These wonderful interviews grant readers access to some of the world's most unique and uniquely insightful icons. Time and again, Jensen shows us how his subjects' graciousness isn't the result of their success, but the source of it. There's a beautiful, powerful lesson on every page—the kind of rare inspiration for which you'll be thanking your lucky stars."

—Bret Anthony Johnston, author of *Corpus Christi: Stories* and director of creative writing, Harvard University

"This book totally rocks! What a perfect reminder for the everyday human being that the stars and celebrities we look up to most are humans just like us, coming from their own trials and tribulations, triumphs and tests. Wait a second . . . if real humans like them can do it, then that means real humans like *us* can do it, too! I am grateful to see the humanity within all people as we share in what makes our hearts most grateful and celebrate the miracle of life that is. What a great spiritual pick-me-up. Read it! Do it! Just do it!"

—Brad Morris, co-creator of Cowabunga Life!, The GratiDudes, and The Gratitude Dance

"How wonderful to see what those who have achieved fame are grateful for and what an example it is for us, our friends, and our children."

—Tatiana Androsov, president/executive director, Center of American and World Thanksgiving

index

about the author

Todd Aaron Jensen is an award-winning journalist with featured bylines in more than 100 publications around the world, including *GQ*, *Esquire*, *American Way*, *Spirit*, *Razor*, *Moving Pictures*, and *Costco Connection*. His work is syndicated in more than sixty countries. A yoga instructor, foster parent, youth baseball coach, and former high school teacher, Jensen lives in Los Angeles with his wife and their enormous family—which they dub "the twenty-first century Brady Bunch." He is a very grateful man.